Substance Abuse

Recent Titles in
Q&A Health Guides

SUBSTANCE ABUSE

❖

Your Questions Answered

Romeo Vitelli

Q&A Health Guides

GREENWOOD™

An Imprint of ABC-CLIO, LLC
Santa Barbara, California • Denver, Colorado

Library of Congress Cataloging-in-Publication Data

Names: Vitelli, Romeo, author.
Title: Substance abuse / Romeo Vitelli.
Description: Santa Barbara : Greenwood, [2018] | Series: Recent titles in
    Q&A health guides | Includes bibliographical references and index. |
Identifiers: LCCN 2018005414 (print) | LCCN 2018021730 (ebook) | ISBN
    9781440860560 (ebook) | ISBN 9781440860553 (alk. paper)
Subjects: LCSH: Teenagers—Substance use—Treatment. | Teenagers—Drug
    use—Treatment. | Substance abuse—Treatment. | Drug abuse—Treatment.
Classification: LCC HV4999.Y68 (ebook) | LCC HV4999.Y68 V58 2018
    (print) | DDC 613.8—dc23
LC record available at https://lccn.loc.gov/2018005414

ISBN: 978-1-4408-6055-3 (print)
        978-1-4408-6056-0 (ebook)

22 21 20 19 18   1 2 3 4 5

This book is also available as an eBook.

Greenwood
An Imprint of ABC-CLIO, LLC

ABC-CLIO, LLC
130 Cremona Drive, P.O. Box 1911
Santa Barbara, California 93116-1911
www.abc-clio.com

This book is printed on acid-free paper ∞

Manufactured in the United States of America

This book is dedicated to Christina, Laura, Erica, and Anthony: the next generation. It is also dedicated to all of my substance-abusing clients, both within the prison system and in the community, and I thank you for the insights you provided. May this book help others find a way to overcome their addiction problems and stay clean.

Contents

Series Foreword

All of us have questions about our health. Is this normal? Should I be doing something differently? Whom should I talk to about my concerns? And our modern world is full of answers. Thanks to the Internet, there's a wealth of information at our fingertips, from forums where people can share their personal experiences to Wikipedia articles to the full text of medical studies. But finding the right information can be an intimidating and difficult task—some sources are written at too high a level, others have been oversimplified, while still others are heavily biased or simply inaccurate.

Q&A Health Guides address the needs of readers who want accurate, concise answers to their health questions, authored by reputable and objective experts, and written in clear and easy-to-understand language. This series focuses on the topics that matter most to young adult readers, including various aspects of physical and emotional well-being as well as other components of a healthy lifestyle. These guides will also serve as a valuable tool for parents, school counselors, and others who may need to answer teens' health questions.

All books in the series follow the same format to make finding information quick and easy. Each volume begins with an essay on health literacy and why it is so important when it comes to gathering and evaluating health information. Next, the top five myths and misconceptions that surround the topic are dispelled. The heart of each guide is a collection of questions and answers, organized thematically. A selection of five case studies provides real-world examples to illuminate key concepts. Rounding out each volume are a directory of resources, glossary, and index.

It is our hope that the books in this series will not only provide valuable information but will also help guide readers toward a lifetime of healthy decision making.

Acknowledgments

I would like to thank the various researchers and therapists whose efforts helped make this book possible. Thanks also go to Maxine Taylor of ABC-CLIO and their excellent support staff as well as those colleagues of mine who were kind enough to review sections of this book and provide helpful suggestions on how it could be improved.

Introduction

> At the bottom of every person's dependency, there is always pain. Discovering the pain and healing it is an essential step in ending dependency.
> —Chris Prentiss, *The Alcoholism and Addiction Cure*

Whitney Houston, Robin Williams, Amy Winehouse, Philip Seymour Hoffman, John Belushi, and so on, the roster of famous people whose deaths have been linked to drug or alcohol abuse seems endless. But they are just the tip of the iceberg considering how pervasive drug and alcohol abuse continues to be around the world.

Whether we are talking about alcohol, barbiturates, ecstasy, cocaine, heroin, morphine (along with all of the other opioids), amphetamines, or the host of designer drugs being introduced on a regular basis, substance abuse continues to be a global epidemic affecting every country on Earth. In 2015 alone, available statistics report 307,400 deaths worldwide from substance use though the true number of drug- and alcohol-related deaths that occur each year seems impossible to know for certain.

But the true economic and social impact of substance abuse is far greater. Though many substance abusers seem able to function to some extent despite their dependence issues, the financial and social costs linked to substance abuse can be astronomical. They can include lost work days, an overburdened health-care system, automobile accidents, workplace injuries, violent crime associated with substance use, and the costs of police, courts, and prisons. But an even greater cost can arise from the emotional impact substance abuse can have on addicts and their extended families—a legacy that can last for generations.

According to the *Diagnostic and Statistical Manual of Mental Disorders* and the International Statistical Classification of Disease and Related Health Problems, *substance abuse* refers to the psychological or physical harm resulting from overusing any addictive substance.

And there are a staggering range of addictive substances out there, including alcohol, narcotics, prescription pain medications, antianxiety and antidepressant medications, hallucinogens, stimulants, depressants, party drugs, and designer drugs, as well as even more controversial options such as tobacco, caffeine, and cannabis.

Still, there is nothing really new about drug or alcohol abuse, which, in a real sense, may even be older than the human race. Animal researchers have turned up countless examples of animals observed in the wild becoming "stoned," including cats and their catnip, cows eating loco grass, bees becoming intoxicated on orchid nectar, and birds consuming poppy seeds.

In Africa, birthplace of our species, virtually all known primate species have been observed eating the roots of the iboga plant—source of the powerful alkaloid ibogaine. According to Ronald Siegel, author of the classic 1989 book *Intoxication: The Universal Drive for Mind-Altering Substances*, the need to become stoned on mind-altering substances may well be a universal motivator in all living organisms.

That certainly seems to be the case for humans, considering that our history of psychoactive substance use stretches far back into prehistoric times. Even a superficial glance at the herbal remedies developed by shamans and traditional healers around the world shows a long list of hallucinogenic and mind-altering substances used for spiritual, recreational, and healing purposes.

Some of the oldest examples of world literature include references to fermented fruit juices, sacred herbs, and medicinal remedies aimed at conquering pain, enabling spirit quests, and simple enjoyment. From the Lotus Eaters of Homer's *Odyssey*; the Dionysian Mysteries of ancient Greece; references to soma and other mind-altering substances in the Rig Veda and the Bible; and the popularity of khat, ayahuasca, psilocybin mushrooms, coca leaves, and marijuana in different cultures, there is no questioning the long and varied legacy linked to drugs and alcohol.

But for almost as long as there have been psychoactive substances, there has been evidence for addiction and the medical and social problems that they cause. Many of the ancient medical texts describe symptoms that would hardly be out of place in any modern addiction clinic. In a very real sense, drug and alcohol use has been a significant part of the history of the world we know today and continues to shape the economy and politics of every country on Earth.

Considering how common substance abuse really is and how far-reaching its effects are, the need for better prevention and treatment options to help substance abusers and their families is plain enough. Unfortunately, along with well-meaning government policies that often do more harm than good, there are still far too many misconceptions about substance abuse, often spread by well-meaning friends and family members, as well as through the Internet, that add to the burden many substance abusers and their families face.

In my new book *Substance Abuse: Your Questions Answered*, I debunk some of the misconceptions about substance abuse and discuss how damaging these widely held beliefs can be. The book answers many of the most common questions people are likely to ask about substance abuse and is broken down into different sections to help readers focus on what is most important to them. The sections are General Information; Causes and Risk Factors; Consequences of Substance Abuse; Culture, Media, and Substance Abuse; Treatment, Prevention, and Life after Substance Abuse. Along with case studies exploring different aspects of substance abuse, a Directory of Resources is provided for people seeking additional information.

This book is intended to provide basic information to anyone whose life has been affected by drug or alcohol abuse, whether they are the substance abusers themselves, concerned friends, family members, teachers, or treatment professionals. Though written in commonsense language for anyone to understand, a glossary is also provided for any technical terms you may not recognize.

For far too many substance abusers and their families, there is often a sense of pessimism that comes from the idea that addicts are incapable of breaking free of their addiction. This is far from the case, however, as countless success stories have shown, some of which is mentioned in this book. The most critical thing to remember is that the right help is out there; you just need to be willing to find it.

Good luck!

Guide to Health Literacy

On her 13th birthday, Samantha was diagnosed with type 2 diabetes. She consulted her mom and her aunt, both of whom also have type 2 diabetes, and decided to go with their strategy of managing diabetes by taking insulin. As a result of participating in an after-school program at her middle school that focused on health literacy, she learned that she can help manage the level of glucose in her bloodstream by counting her carbohydrate intake, following a diabetic diet, and exercising regularly. But, what exactly should she do? How does she keep track of her carbohydrate intake? What is a diabetic diet? How long should she exercise and what type of exercise should she do? Samantha is a visual learner, so she turned to her favorite source of media, YouTube, to answer these questions. She found videos from individuals around the world sharing their experiences and tips, doctors (or at least people who have "Dr." in their YouTube channel names), government agencies such as the National Institutes of Health, and even video clips from cat lovers who have cats with diabetes. With guidance from the librarian and the health and science teachers at her school, she assessed the credibility of the information in these videos and even compared their suggestions to some of the print resources that she was able to find at her school library. Now, she knows exactly how to count her carbohydrate level, how to prepare and follow a diabetic diet, and how much (and what) exercise is needed daily. She intends to share her findings with her mom and her aunt, and now she wants to create a chart that summarizes what she has learned that she can share with her doctor.

Samantha's experience is not unique. She represents a shift in our society; an individual no longer views himself or herself as a passive recipient of medical care but as an active mediator of his or her own health. However, in this era when any individual can post his or her opinions and experiences with a particular health condition online with just a few clicks or publish a memoir, it is vital that people know how to assess the credibility of health information. Gone are the days when "publishing" health information required intense vetting. The health information landscape is highly saturated, and people have innumerable sources where they can find information about practically any health topic. The sources (whether print, online, or a person) that an individual consults for health information are crucial because the accuracy and trustworthiness of the information can potentially affect his or her overall health. The ability to find, select, assess, and use health information constitutes a type of literacy—health literacy—that everyone must possess.

THE DEFINITION AND PHASES OF HEALTH LITERACY

One of the most popular definitions for health literacy comes from Ratzan and Parker (2000), who describe health literacy as "the degree to which individuals have the capacity to obtain, process, and understand basic health information and services needed to make appropriate health decisions." Recent research has extrapolated health literacy into health literacy bits, further shedding light on the multiple phases and literacy practices that are embedded within the multifaceted concept of health literacy. Although this research has focused primarily on online health information seeking, these health literacy bits are needed to successfully navigate both print and online sources. There are six phases of health information seeking: (1) Information Need Identification and Question Formulation, (2) Information Search, (3) Information Comprehension, (4) Information Assessment, (5) Information Management, and (6) Information Use.

The first phase is the *information need identification and question formulation phase*. In this phase, one needs to be able to develop and refine a range of questions to frame one's search and understand relevant health terms. In the second phase, *information search*, one has to possess appropriate searching skills, such as using proper keywords and correct spelling in search terms, especially when using search engines and databases. It is also crucial to understand how search engines work (i.e., how search results are derived, what the order of the search results means, how to use the snippets that are provided in the search results list to select websites, and how to determine which listings are ads on a search engine results page). One also has to limit reliance on surface characteristics, such as the design of a website or a book (a website or book that appears to have a lot of information or looks aesthetically pleasant does not necessarily mean it has good information) and language used (a website or book that utilizes jargon, the keywords that one used to conduct the search, or the word "information" does not necessarily indicate it will have good information). The next phase is *information comprehension*, whereby one needs to have the ability to read, comprehend, and recall the information (including textual, numerical, and visual content) one has located from the books and/or online resources.

To assess the credibility of health information (*information assessment* phase), one needs to be able to evaluate information for accuracy, evaluate how current the information is (e.g., when a website was last updated or when a book was published), and evaluate the creators of the source—for example, examine site sponsors or type of sites (.com, .gov, .edu, or .org) or the author of a book (practicing doctor, a celebrity doctor, a patient of a specific disease, etc.) to determine the believability of the person/ organization providing the information. Such credibility perceptions tend to become generalized, so they must be frequently reexamined (e.g., the belief that a specific news agency always has credible health information needs continuous vetting). One also needs to evaluate the credibility of the medium (e.g., television, Internet, radio, social media, and book) and evaluate—not just accept without questioning—others' claims regarding the validity of a site, book, or other specific source of information. At this stage, one has to "make sense of information gathered from diverse sources by identifying misconceptions, main and supporting ideas, con-flicting information, point of view, and biases" (American Association of School Librarians [AASL], 2009, p. 13) and conclude which sources/ information are valid and accurate by using conscious strategies rather than simply using intuitive judgments or "rules of thumb." This phase is the most challenging segment of health information seeking and serves as a determinant of success (or lack thereof) in the information-seeking process. The following section on Sources of Health Information further explains this phase.

The fifth phase is *information management*, whereby one has to orga-nize information that has been gathered in some manner to ensure easy retrieval and use in the future. The last phase is *information use*, in which one will synthesize information found across various resources, draw conclusions, and locate the answer to one's original question and/or the content that fulfills the information need. This phase also often involves implementation, such as using the information to solve a health problem; make health-related decisions; identify and engage in behaviors that will help a person to avoid health risks; share the health information found with family members and friends who may benefit from it; and advocate more broadly for personal, family, or community health.

THE IMPORTANCE OF HEALTH LITERACY

The conception of health has moved from a passive view (someone is either well or ill) to one that is more active and process based (someone is working toward preventing or managing disease). Hence, the dominant focus has shifted from doctors and treatments to patients and prevention, resulting in the need to strengthen our ability and confidence (as patients and consumers of health care) to look for, assess, understand, manage, share, adapt, and use health-related information. An individual's health literacy level has been found to predict his or her health status better than age, race, educational attainment, employment status, and income level (National Network of Libraries of Medicine, 2013). Greater health literacy also enables individuals to better communicate with health-care providers such as doctors, nutritionists, and therapists, as they can pose more relevant, informed, and useful questions to health-care providers. Another added advantage of greater health literacy is better information-seeking skills, not only for health but also in other domains, such as completing assignments for school.

SOURCES OF HEALTH INFORMATION: THE GOOD, THE BAD, AND THE IN-BETWEEN

For generations, doctors, nurses, nutritionists, health coaches, and other health professionals have been the trusted sources of health information. Additionally, researchers have found that young adults, when they have health-related questions, typically turn to a family member who has had firsthand experience with a health condition because of their family member's close proximity and because of their past experience with, and trust in, this individual. Expertise should be a core consideration when consulting a person, website, or book for health information. The credentials and background of the person or author and conflicting interests of the author (and his or her organization) must be checked and validated to ensure the likely credibility of the health information he or she is conveying. While books often have implied credibility because of the peer-review process involved, self-publishing has challenged this credibility, so qualifications of book authors should also be verified. When it comes to health information, currency of the source must also be examined. When examining health information/studies presented, pay attention to the exhaustiveness of research methods utilized to offer recommendations or conclusions. Small and nondiverse sample size is often—but not always—an indication of reduced credibility. Studies that confuse correlation with causation is another potential issue to watch for. Information seekers must also pay attention to the sponsors of the research studies. For example, if a study is sponsored by manufacturers of drug Y and the study recommends that drug Y is the best treatment to manage or cure a disease, this may indicate a lack of objectivity on the part of the researchers.

The Internet is rapidly becoming one of the main sources of health information. Online forums, news agencies, personal blogs, social media sites, pharmacy sites, and celebrity "doctors" are all offering medical and health information targeted at various types of people in regard to all types of diseases and symptoms. There are professional journalists, citizen journalists, hoaxers, and people paid to write fake health news on various sites that may appear to have a legitimate domain name and may even have authors who claim to have professional credentials, such as an MD. All these sites *may* offer useful information or information that appears to be useful and relevant; however, much of the information may be debatable and may fall into gray areas that require readers to discern credibility, reliability, and biases.

While broad recognition and acceptance of certain media, institutions, and people often serve as the most popular determining factors to assess credibility of health information among young people, keep in mind that there are legitimate Internet sites, databases, and books that publish health information and serve as sources of health information for doctors, other health sites, and members of the public. For example, MedlinePlus (https://medlineplus.gov) has trusted sources on over 975 diseases and conditions and presents the information in easy-to-understand language.

The chart here presents factors to consider when assessing credibility of health information. However, keep in mind that these factors function only as a guide and require continuous updating to keep abreast with the changes in the landscape of health information, information sources, and technologies.

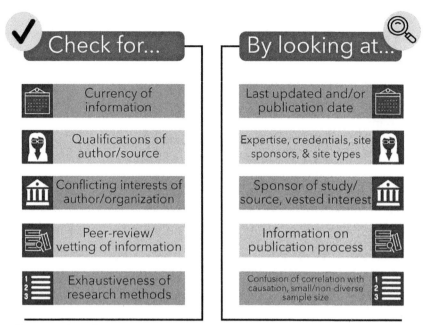

All images from flaticon.com

The chart can serve as a guide; however, approaching a librarian about how one can go about assessing the credibility of both print and online health information is far more effective than using generic checklist-type tools. While librarians are not health experts, they can apply and teach patrons strategies to determine the credibility of health information.

With the prevalence of fake sites and fake resources that appear to be legitimate, it is important to use the following health information assessment tips to verify health information that one has obtained (St. Jean et al., 2015, p. 151):

- **Don't assume you are right**: Even when you feel very sure about an answer, keep in mind that the answer may not be correct, and it is important to conduct (further) searches to validate the information.
- **Don't assume you are wrong**: You may actually have correct information, even if the information you encounter does not match—that is, you may be right and the resources that you have found may contain false information.
- **Take an open approach**: Maintain a critical stance by not including your preexisting beliefs as keywords (or letting them influence your

choice of keywords) in a search, as this may influence what it is possible to find out.

*   **Verify, verify, and verify**: Information found, especially on the Internet, needs to be validated, no matter how the information appears on the site (i.e., regardless of the appearance of the site or the quantity of information that is included).

Health literacy comes with experience navigating health information. Professional sources of health information, such as doctors, health-care providers, and health databases, are still the best, but one also has the power to search for health information and then verify it by consulting with these trusted sources and by using the health information assessment tips and guide shared previously.

Mega Subramaniam, PhD
Associate Professor, College of Information Studies,
University of Maryland

REFERENCES AND FURTHER READING

American Association of School Librarians (AASL). (2009). *Standards for the 21st-century learner in action*. Chicago, IL: American Association of School Librarians.

Hilligoss, B., & Rieh, S.-Y. (2008). Developing a unifying framework of credibility assessment: Construct, heuristics, and interaction in context. *Information Processing & Management, 44*(4), 1467–1484.

Kuhlthau, C. C. (1988). Developing a model of the library search process: Cognitive and affective aspects. *Reference Quarterly, 28*(2), 232–242.

National Network of Libraries of Medicine (NNLM). (2013). Health literacy. Bethesda, MD: National Network of Libraries of Medicine. Retrieved from nnlm.gov/outreach/consumer/hlthlit.html

Ratzan, S. C., & Parker, R. M. (2000). Introduction. In C. R. Selden, M. Zorn, S. C. Ratzan, & R. M. Parker (Eds.), *National Library of Medicine current bibliographies in medicine: Health literacy*. NLM Publication No. CBM 2000-1. Bethesda, MD: National Institutes of Health, U.S. Department of Health and Human Services.

St. Jean, B., Subramaniam, M., Taylor, N. G., Follman, R., Kodama, C., & Casciotti, D. (2015). The influence of positive hypothesis testing on youths' online health-related information seeking. *New Library World, 116*(3/4), 136–154.

St. Jean, B., Taylor, N.G., Kodama, C., & Subramaniam, M. (February 2017). Assessing the health information source perceptions of tweens using card-sorting exercises. *Journal of Information Science.* Retrieved from http://journals.sagepub.com/doi/abs/10.1177/0165551516687728

Subramaniam, M., St. Jean, B., Taylor, N.G., Kodama, C., Follman, R., & Casciotti, D. (2015). Bit by bit: Using design-based research to improve the health literacy of adolescents. *JMIR Research Protocols,* 4(2), paper e62. Retrieved from http://www.ncbi.nlm.nih.gov/pmc/articles/PMC4464334/

Valenza, J. (2016, November 26). Truth, truthiness, and triangulation: A news literacy toolkit for a "post-truth" world [Web log]. Retrieved from http://blogs.slj.com/neverendingsearch/2016/11/26/truth-truthiness-triangulation-and-the-librarian-way-a-news-literacy-toolkit-for-a-post-truth-world/

Common Misconceptions
about Substance Abuse

1. SUBSTANCE ABUSE IS THE SAME AS DRUG ABUSE

According to most drug authorities, any substance can be addictive if it has psychoactive effects, can promote a self-reinforcing pattern of use, and can lead to cravings and unpleasant physiological effects following withdrawal. While these symptoms are most commonly associated with well-known drugs such as heroin and cocaine, there are many other substances that are also prime candidates for abuse. Alcohol is probably the most addictive substance known though it remains perfectly legal in most places. Nicotine and caffeine are also potentially addictive substances that are legal in most places despite the difficulty in quitting and potential for health problems. Cannabis is also addictive though this is more controversial and, as we will see later in the book, is rapidly gaining legal acceptance in many places both for medical and recreational use. For more information about the most commonly abused substances, see Question 3.

2. PEOPLE CAN'T BECOME ADDICTED TO PRESCRIPTION DRUGS

When properly prescribed and under medical supervision, the risk of prescription drug addiction is relatively small. Still, when treating conditions such as chronic pain, medical doctors need to balance the risk of addiction with the patient's need for relief, which can often be diffi-cult. Medical doctors need to monitor how their patients use these med-ications and take action when concerns arise. This usually occurs when patients take more medication than prescribed or mix their medications with other potentially addictive substances such as alcohol or recreational drugs. They may also attempt "doctor shopping" to get prescription medi-cations from other doctors for the same conditions. For this reason, many jurisdictions have set up patient registries to prevent potential abuse. See Question 14 for further details.

3. ONLY ILLEGAL DRUGS ARE DANGEROUS

While drugs such as heroin and cocaine have a long history, new "designer drugs" are continually being introduced, which are relatively unknown except as new ways for people to get high. Unfortunately, because these drugs are so new, existing drug laws can't enforce their use and they remain technically legal until the law is changed. Since most of these drugs have unknown side effects, the potential for serious medical issues, and even death, remains disturbingly high. And then there are the "legal" drugs such as alcohol and tobacco which, despite being extremely addic-tive, can often be consumed without any legal consequences (unless they are consumed by minors or used while driving). Since drug laws are in a continual state of change, they are typically not a good indicator of which drugs can be consumed safely. This is why it is so important to stay well informed and to practice good judgment about any potentially mind-altering substance, especially if a friend or acquaintance assures you that it's "perfectly safe and legal." For more information about how socie-tal attitudes impact patterns of substance abuse, see Question 30.

4. DRUG AND ALCOHOL ABUSERS ARE UNTREATABLE

While overcoming drug and alcohol addiction can be horrendously dif-ficult, especially for long-time abusers, it *is* possible as countless success stories can attest. But many of these same success stories also show how important it is to form support networks that can help with the often trau-matic process of getting clean. The phrase "no man is an island" definitely applies for people trying to overcome substance abuse, and emotional support, whether from friends, family members, or treatment profession-als, can be vital. Still, while there are numerous treatment alternatives out there (and we will discuss them further in this book), there is no one pathway to overcoming drug or alcohol abuse. Many users may find themselves trying different forms of treatments before settling on one that works best for them. Whatever treatment is used, the most important step is not to give in to despair, particularly when relapses occur (and they will). The section of this book on treatment, particularly Questions 38, 40, 41, 43, 45, and 46, explores options in more detail.

5. DRUG OR ALCOHOL ABUSE IS NOT A DISEASE, JUST A LACK OF WILLPOWER

This is one of the most heartbreaking misconceptions faced by people dealing with substance abuse. Many otherwise well-meaning people have difficulty accepting that substance abuse is a disease and feel that abusers are somehow guilty of lacking the willpower to quit rather than suffering from a medical condition. Whether due to genetics, upbringing, poor environment, or emotional problems stemming from trauma, many people are particularly vulnerable to substance abuse, and moralizing about their lack of control makes the process of getting clean much harder than it needs to be. As you will see in later sections of this book, drug and alcohol addiction is linked to systematic changes in brain chemistry and neural pathways as people become more acclimatized to substance use. Substance use also affects the reward systems of the brain and often leads to physical dependency as a result. This is what makes quitting so difficult for many people and why trying to rely exclusively on willpower rarely works for long. For more information about how substance abuse affects the brain, see Question 23.

QUESTIONS AND ANSWERS

General Information

1. What is substance abuse and dependence?

According to one common definition, substance abuse is the "overde-pendence on a psychoactive substance leading to a systematic pattern of dependence." Formerly referred to as "drug abuse," the term "sub-stance abuse" has become more common since it includes psychoactive substances that are legal in many places, such as alcohol, caffeine, and tobacco.

For that matter, even the term "abuse" can be hard to pin down since it often depends on how frequently the abuse occurs and the impact it has on quality of life. In his 2004 book *Illegal Drugs*, physician Paul Gahlinger describes four levels of abuse. He calls the first level "experimental use" since it typically involves people "experimenting" with a psychoactive substance for the first time. Whether that substance is alcohol, canna-bis, tobacco, or some other drug, many users may decide that their initial experience is enough and stop at this stage. The next level, according to Gahlinger, is "recreational use." People may simply choose to "dabble" in a particular substance on an occasional basis, but their lives are not being disrupted in any significant way as a result. This can include most casual users of alcohol, cannabis, or tobacco, who rarely move on to more severe substance use.

Gahlinger's third level is what he terms "circumstantial use," such as when substance use follows a certain predictable pattern. People who commonly drink or use drugs during social occasions or who take substances as a way of coping with stress are usually considered circumstantial users since they are not necessarily experiencing health problems and their substance use is usually fairly limited (at first). Still, this kind of circumstantial use leaves them particularly vulnerable to Gahlinger's fourth level: "compulsive use." This involves forming a dependence on drugs or alcohol that can lead to serious psychological or physiological problems.

According to the most recent edition of the *Diagnostic and Statistical Manual of Mental Disorders* (DSM-V), signs of *dependence* can include a strong desire to keep taking the addictive substance; difficulty in controlling the urge to keep using despite a desire to quit; persisting in using the substance despite knowing about harmful consequences; giving a higher priority to substance use over other, healthier activities; and, in many cases, increased tolerance and potential withdrawal symptoms when the substance use is stopped.

The *DSM-V* identifies 10 separate classes of substances that can lead to addiction: alcohol, caffeine, cannabis, hallucinogens, inhalants (including glue and solvents), opioids such as heroin and morphine, sedatives (including hypnotics and anxiolytics), stimulants, tobacco, and other (or unknown) substances. As you can see, this list is open ended since new psychoactive substances continue to come along with all the legal, ethical, and medical issues that go with them.

All of the addictive substances on this list act through direct stimulation of the brain's reward system, which is normally involved in the processes linked to pleasure, the ability to learn new behaviors, and the formation of new memories. Since addictive substances can produce a chemical "high" that is often greater than what the brain can achieve on its own, prolonged use results in a pattern of dependence that can often override normal reward activities.

While the *DSM* recognizes other forms of addiction, including gambling and sex addiction, the term "substance disorder" specifically deals with the cognitive, behavioral, and medical issues associated with abusing psychoactive substances. The *DSM* also draws a distinction between *substance use disorders*, which we usually think of as drug or alcohol addiction, and *substance-induced disorders*, which are medical conditions that can result from chronic drug or alcohol use. Substance-induced disorders can include intoxication and withdrawal effects as well as many of the neurological and cognitive problems associated with them.

There are a wide range of different psychiatric diagnoses that can also be linked to different kinds of substance use and how prolonged use can affect people over time. For example, alcohol use disorder typically involves chronic alcohol use despite a persistent desire to quit or repeated failures to do so; physical cravings; neglect of other important activities such as work, school, or family responsibilities; and increasing tolerance and withdrawal effects (more on tolerance and withdrawal in Question 2).

The sheer range of physiological, cognitive, and behavioral symptoms linked to different kinds of drug and alcohol use could fill an encyclopedia and extends far beyond the scope of this book. Some of these symptoms will be covered in more detail in Questions 4 and 5.

2. What is the difference between physiological and psychological dependence?

The pattern of dependence linked to substance abuse can take different forms depending on the symptoms being displayed and how they affect a user's mental and physical well-being. To understand the different ways that addiction can occur, substance abuse treatment professionals often distinguish between *physical* and *psychological* dependence.

Physical dependence refers to the changes that occur in the body with chronic overuse of different kinds of psychoactive substances. Among the substances linked to physiological dependence are alcohol; all types of opioids including heroin, morphine, and oxycodone; barbiturates, benzodiazepines; and many psychiatric medications.

Over time, the brain and the central nervous system adapt to chemical changes caused by chronic substance use until reaching the point of requiring larger doses to have the same psychoactive effect. Along with this increased tolerance come the physiological symptoms that can occur during drug withdrawal or even when the regular dosage is lowered. How severe the withdrawal symptoms are often varies according to the substance used, the extent of the abuse, and the kind of treatment being received during the withdrawal period.

Withdrawal symptoms can include nausea, vomiting, rapid heart rate, diarrhea, hypertension, sweating, and tremors. While most of these symptoms are relatively mild, more severe withdrawal symptoms can also occur. Anyone experiencing auditory or visual hallucinations, seizures, mental confusion, or convulsions should seek emergency medical treatment immediately since these symptoms are often life threatening.

Since many prescription medications can also lead to tolerance and withdrawal issues, medical doctors prescribing drugs that can cause physiological dependence need to advise their patients about the potential risks associated with their continued use. They also need to monitor their patient's drug use, including potential interaction effects these medications might have with other medications. Many jurisdictions are becoming more aware of the central role that physicians can play and often require them to report any patients who are showing problems with addiction.

Psychological dependence stems from regarding psychoactive substance as a "crutch" that becomes part of a person's way of coping with stress or emotional upset. Over time, many users may find that they lose the ability to manage their emotions naturally and need to rely on their drug of choice to remain calm or stress free. This often leads to a purely psychological form of withdrawal if their drug use is disrupted in any way. Symptoms of psychological withdrawal can include anxiety, a reduced ability to feel pleasure (anhedonia), panic attacks, and general unease.

As one example of psychological abuse of a substance, many people using sleep medications may find themselves becoming overdependent on their medication to the point of being unable to sleep whenever this medication is unavailable. This is why medical doctors prefer to prescribe sleep medications only as a short-term solution to insomnia. Other kinds of addictions, including gambling or sexual addiction, are examples of psychological dependence that often require treatment to help people control their withdrawal symptoms and overcome their need for a new "fix."

In a real sense, psychological addiction can occur with any substance or behavior and can be especially dangerous since many people refuse to believe that a nonphysiological addiction is possible.

Though psychological and physiological dependence tend to be seen as separate forms of addictions, they really aren't. Chronic substance abusers will often experience psychological dependence as well as physiological dependence due to long-term use. For example, chronic alcoholics may come to depend on their drinking to cope with stress, loneliness, or other emotional issues and, when their drinking is disrupted, often experience psychological distress in addition to the physiological withdrawal symptoms. As a result, the alcohol itself becomes a way of coping with the health and lifestyle problems chronic alcoholics typically face. This is what makes going "cold turkey" so hazardous for drug and alcohol abusers and also why relapses occur so frequently.

Substance abusers need to be particularly aware of the psychological and physiological aspects of addiction and what it can mean for attempts at quitting. Never assume you can do it on your own.

3. What are the most commonly abused substances?

This is another tricky question to answer given how many different psychoactive substances can be obtained perfectly legally. Caffeine can be found in tea, coffee, many soft drinks, a surprising array of candies and other confectionaries, and even in many medications. While legislation requires all products containing caffeine to include information on caffeine levels, there are no real limits on how much caffeine the average person might choose to consume on a daily basis. Though the amount of caffeine needed to cause serious medical problems is far greater than what people are likely to consume daily, that's not the same as saying that it's completely harmless either.

After caffeine, the next most-abused drug is alcohol. Despite having a wide range of other uses, including as an antiseptic, for preserving specimens in laboratories, as an antifreeze, and even to fuel automobiles, alcoholic beverages have been around since ancient times. Also, as you can see from Question 5, alcohol has been linked to millions of deaths worldwide each year, and consumer surveys estimate that nearly 90 percent of all adults admit to drinking at some point in their lives. Legal in most places, alcohol remains the drug of choice for countless people worldwide, and that seems unlikely to change in the near-future.

After caffeine and alcohol, nicotine is the next most popular psychoactive substance worldwide. A potent stimulant found in the nightshade family of plants, nicotine is most commonly found in tobacco plants. With a history dating back thousands of years in Central and South America, tobacco has become a major cash crop despite the growing evidence for the harmful effects that nicotine can have. Much like other drugs, nicotine use can lead to tolerance and withdrawal effects, not to mention being toxic at high-enough levels. Even with education campaigns warning about its dangers, nicotine abuse remains a major health risk, largely because it remains legal in most places.

For most people, however, the term "drug use" is usually seen as applying strictly to narcotics or other illegal psychoactive substances. According to the 2016 Global Drug Survey, the 10 most commonly abused substances (after caffeine, alcohol, and tobacco products) are:

- Cannabis, including marijuana, hashish, and synthetic cannabinoids
- MDMA (ecstasy)
- Cocaine (including crack cocaine)
- Amphetamines (cover most stimulants including "speed")
- Lysergic acid diethylamide (LSD)
- Psilocybin (hallucinogenic mushrooms)

- Prescribed and nonprescribed opioid medication
- Nitrous oxide
- Ketamine
- Amyl nitrate (poppers)

Though the effects of most of these different drugs are already well known, new drugs are also becoming available. Whether they begin as legitimate pharmaceuticals that get diverted for recreational use or are created in illegal laboratories, the health dangers these new drugs pose are only beginning to be understood. And since it takes time for legislation curbing these drugs to be drafted and voted on, many of these new drugs are often legal since they can't be covered under existing laws, which makes it more imperative than ever that substance abusers be aware of the serious dangers that they face when consuming an unknown substance.

4. What are some of the most common signs of substance addiction?

Though there are a wide range of psychoactive substances and the pattern of abuse is often different, certain signs are being commonly seen in substance abusers, especially when the substance use is out of control. These signs can include:

Uncharacteristic mood swings, apathy, or aggressive behavior—Substance abusers typically begin using their drug of choice as a way to handle stress or to experience positive emotions. As their tolerance builds up, however, they often need to consume more and more of the same substance to get the same benefit they experienced before. They may also begin to experience withdrawal effects, whether of the physiological or psychological variety, which can lead to drastic "highs" and "lows" in their mood state depending on where they happen to be in their regular pattern of use.

What can result has been described as an emotional roller-coaster as the substance abuser's mood shifts from happy, self-confident, and tranquil to being drained, apathetic, irritable, or withdrawn. Since this shift can be extremely rapid, family and friends can often be caught by surprise, especially when the abuser begins lashing out, whether physically or verbally. Still, this kind of emotional volatility can also be a symptom of mental health problems, being a victim of bullying or other social issues, or even adolescent hormones at work, so parents and teachers need to investigate further to determine what is really happening.

Chronic truancy or lateness for school or work—This is a little trickier since most users are able to keep their substance use hidden, at least in the early stages. Still, as problems develop, they may try to conceal what is happening by inventing excuses such as feeling sick or faking an emergency to avoid having to face other people until they can make themselves appear more normal.

Personal neglect—As users experience problems with withdrawal or side effects, they may not have the energy or desire to maintain their personal appearance. Failing to change their clothes, neglecting basic hygiene, or grooming can be an important warning sign since it might mean that they are on the verge of more severe health problems. Again, this kind of personal neglect can also be seen in people with mental health problems, so it doesn't occur only with substance abusers.

Attempting to cover suspicious behavior through lying or being vague—For users with regular commitments, including work or school, it often becomes increasingly difficult to meet these responsibilities due to their substance use. Many users may come up with different excuses or simply be vague about why they are making mistakes or failing to meet deadlines. This can also lead to worsening relationships with teachers, employers, family members, or friends.

Apathy, loss of motivation, and marked changes in regular habits—Any abrupt change in routine, whether it involves losing interest in regular hobbies or apparent loss of interest in long-term goals, is a potential sign of substance abuse. For many substance users, the need to pursue a new high or prevent withdrawal can often seem more important than just about anything else. While this can also be a sign of potential mental illness or trauma, it certainly needs to be investigated further.

Depression, shyness, and/or social anxiety—Since many users rely on drugs or alcohol to medicate away other problems they may be experiencing, they may find themselves losing their ability to cope with these problems without self-medicating. On the other hand, certain psychoactive substances may actually *cause* mental health problems due to overuse or withdrawal. Alcohol, for example, can be a strong depressant though most people tend to think of it as a stimulant. Depending on the amount of alcohol consumed, severe depressant effects such as reduced arousal and even full-blown depression can often occur. While proving that certain drugs can lead to depression

or other mental health problems can be difficult, some particular cul-
prits have been identified, including cannabis and amphetamines.

Behavioral signs of drug abuse—Key changes in behavior occur, such as
increased sleepiness or a disrupted sleep schedule, frequent absences
from home, and, in extreme cases, drunken behavior or slurred
speech.

While not all of these signs may not necessarily indicate a substance abuse
problem, the overall pattern often becomes clear enough over time. It is
important for parents or teachers to note that many young people can
show these signs as part of normal adolescent or young adult development. Be careful in how you investigate what is happening, and don't
make accusations without strong evidence.

5. How can substance abusers tell that their abuse is out of control?

Not everyone who uses psychoactive substances will become an addict.
As you can see in Question 1, there are different levels of abuse and people in the early stages may well decide to quit after realizing that drugs or
alcohol isn't for them. For people who progress to hard-core substance
use, it becomes easy to ignore the warning signs discussed in the previous
question due to addiction or simple denial. There are also more serious
indicators that are much harder to ignore:

Conflict with authority figures—Not surprisingly, prolonged substance
use can lead to serious problems when users are confronted by
school administrators, employers, or even police. Since most forms
of substance use are illegal in different places, problems with the law
become unavoidable over time.

Sudden problems with debt or requests for money—Funding a drug or
alcohol habit can be expensive, especially when there is no legal
source that can be used to feed that habit. As tolerance builds up,
the amount of money that needs to be spent increases as well. Once
users exhaust their own financial resources, they often resort to beg-
ging friends and family for money, even if they are vague about why
they need it. After they go into debt, the money they owe often bal-
loons until they are completely incapable of paying down this debt,
which can then lead to stealing.

Stealing from family, friends, or work—Once substance users become desperate enough, stealing money, valuables, or anything else that can be converted into cash becomes common. Though their conscience may bother them at first, they tend to rationalize that nobody would miss what has been taken and, after a while, they may simply stop caring and accept that they will be caught sooner or later.

Selling off personal possessions—Since users will often raise money to feed their habit any way they can, it's hardly uncommon for them to sell off personal possessions, even possessions that may have a great deal of sentimental value or that have brought considerable joy in the past. This can include jewelry, electronic goods, and musical instruments and can often be sold for only a fraction of their true value. They may also sell items belonging to friends or family members in the hope that they will not be caught.

Dealing drugs—For many users desperate for cash, the temptation to sell drugs to raise money for their own habit may be hard to resist. People engaged in drug dealing can often be recognized by their secretive behavior, frequent absences from home or work, and use of drug-related slang.

Medical signs of drug-related health problems—Along with withdrawal, there are various medical signs that someone is abusing drugs. For example, certain drugs can produce eye discoloration such as "red eye," which is seen in many cannabis users. This may prompt users to wear dark glasses to conceal what is happening, even at night or in gloomy weather. Other signs of substance-related medical problems include short-term memory loss, concentration problems, poor motor coordination, impaired judgment, poor appetite, and/ or sudden weight loss. Such weight loss can also lead to a compromised immune system, leaving users much more susceptible to viral and bacterial infections as well as a much longer recovery time from colds or flu. Though these health problems could also be related to other physical or mental health issues, any abrupt appearance of health problems should always be investigated further.

Though any of these signs are serious in themselves, addicts whose substance use is out of control can experience most or all of these signs before seeking help. By this time, the substance abuse has typically reached the point of becoming life threatening and, as a result, the risk of death or serious disability becomes much greater as well.

6. How widespread is substance abuse?

There may be no real way of determining the true extent of substance abuse considering how successful many users are in keeping their substance problems hidden. In a real sense, most available statistics on drug and alcohol abuse worldwide dramatically underestimate how prevalent this problem is in most countries around the world.

According to recent statistics released by the World Health Organization, alcohol abuse alone can account for 3.3 million deaths each year (about 5.9 percent of total deaths) as well as approximately 5.1 percent of the total global burden of disease and injury. When looking at other psychoactive substances, a 2008 survey estimated that 150–250 million people used cannabis, cocaine, or other restricted substances. This amounts to 3.5–5.7 percent of the world's population between the ages of 15 and 64. Cannabis remains the most commonly used substance (with 129–190 million users worldwide), with amphetamines being a close second.

Part of the problem with trying to gauge how prevalent drug and alcohol use really is worldwide is the fact that many countries don't keep accurate statistics, so doing a country-to-country comparison is often impossible. Still, focusing on specific countries can yield some clues about the kinds of problems that drug and alcohol abuse can often cause.

In the United States alone, the total financial cost stemming from tobacco, alcohol, and drug abuse has been placed at $740 billion annually when factoring in lost work productivity, crime, and health-care costs. According to a recent report released by U.S. surgeon general Vivek Murthy, over 66.7 million Americans engage in binge drinking, while 27.1 million Americans are current users of illicit drugs or abusing prescription drugs. This means that almost 8 percent of all Americans meet diagnostic criteria for a substance use disorder according to the *DSM-V*.

Based on a recent Substance Abuse and Mental Health Services Administration's (SAMHSA's) National Survey on Drug Use and Health, there were 23.5 million Americans aged 12 or older who needed some form of substance abuse treatment in 2009 alone. Of those, only 2.6 million, which amounts to 11.6 percent of the total, actually received treatment.

Also according to the SAMHSA survey, alcoholism was the most common form of abuse, accounting for 23.1 percent of all admissions to publicly funded treatment programs. People with combined drug and alcohol addiction were the next highest group at 18.3 percent, while marijuana (17 percent) and heroin (14.1 percent) made up the next highest groups. In terms of age groups, people in the 25–29 age bracket made up the largest percentage of treatment cases (14.8 percent) as opposed to

14.4 percent for the 20–24 age bracket. For substance users under 20 years old, 7.5 percent of treatment patients fell into the 12–17 age range, while only 4.1 percent were aged 18–19.

When looking at substance-related visits to hospital emergency departments, most of the available U.S. data comes from SAMHSA's Drug Abuse Warning Network (DAWN). According to the most recent statistics from DAWN, there were more than 4.9 million drug-related hospital emergency department visits in 2011 alone. While half of these visits involved adverse reactions to prescription drugs, an additional 1.4 million visits involved nonmedical use of pharmaceutical drugs (including prescription and over-the-counter drugs), and over 1.2 million visits involved illegal drugs, Unfortunately, DAWN doesn't collect statistics on emergency room visits due to alcohol alone, but other sources estimate the percentage of alcohol-related visits to be as high as 32 percent or more.

In comparing emergency room visits over time, the overall trend is even more alarming. In 2004, the number of drug-related visits was 2.5 million but, by 2009, this had risen to 4.6 million. That's an increase of 81 percent in just five years. The largest increase involved pain medication such as oxycodone (up by 242.2 percent), alprazolam (148.3 percent increase), and hydrocodone (124.5 percent). For illicit substances, ecstasy or MDMA showed the greatest increase (rising by 123.2 percent).

At the same time however, recent drug statistics looking at substance use in American adolescents (from 8th to 12th grade in particular) is a bit more encouraging. Apart from cannabis, drug and alcohol abuse has dropped to the lowest level recorded since U.S. drug statistics were first collected. For 12th graders in particular, only 14.3 percent are actively using substances such as alcohol, tobacco (include e-cigarettes), heroin and other opioids, cocaine, and methamphetamines. Cannabis use is also down for younger adolescents (grades 8 and 10) though it remains uncertain how recent changes in cannabis legislation may affect these trends in the future.

As you can imagine, these statistics are just the tip of the iceberg in terms of describing how great a role substance abuse can play in countries around the world. We will explore this further in Question 30.

7. How far back in history does substance abuse go?

As you can see from the Introduction, psychoactive substance use may well predate the human race itself. Examples of different animal species becoming "stoned" in the wild due to ingesting psychoactive plants or fermented fruit are certainly well documented and continue to be reported worldwide.

As for human substance abuse, almost all traces of when and where humans first began using these substances appear lost in prehistory. Still, alcoholic beverages of one sort or another can also be found in virtually every culture around the world. The early Sumerians even had a goddess of beer to mark how important it was to their culture. The ancient Greeks had their own god of alcohol, Dionysius, whose worship often took the form of mystery cults allowing men and women to engage in wild behavior while under the influence of alcohol. Even the Bible makes frequent references to alcohol and its intoxicating effects (getting drunk was the first thing Noah did after he landed his ark).

In fact, anthropologist Solomon Katz has even proposed that our progression from hunter-gatherers to early agriculture may well be due to the accidental discovery of beer 10,000 years ago. Why beer, you ask? In tongue-in-cheek fashion, Katz suggests that beer may well be the "food" that lay at the heart of most early civilizations.

The first beer was probably discovered by accident, the product of wild cereal grains such as wheat and barley that had been left forgotten on a shelf somewhere where it could be contaminated with yeast. It was only after drinking this mixture that early man first discovered the mind-altering properties linked to alcohol. Though the alcohol content would have been fairly low, the "buzz" this proto-beer produced would have been enough to motivate early beer drinkers to experiment with new recipes to produce a better product. The same can probably be said for wine given how easily fruit can ferment if left uneaten for too long.

And our history of using other psychoactive substances seems just as ancient. For example, the *Tabernanthe iboga* shrub found in many parts of Africa may very well be one of the first psychoactive plants used by early humans. Long known for its psychoactive properties (the drug ibogaine was first isolated from iboga roots and leaves), numerous Africans continue to use root bark or specially prepared teas made from the plant in religious ceremonies or for traditional healing.

As for other kinds of psychoactive drugs, virtually every human community around the world appears to have developed their own preferred brands more or less independently. Whether in the form of mescaline and peyote in Central and South America, pituri in Australia, kava in parts of the south Pacific, or iboga and qat in Africa, mind-altering drugs were often used for medicine, spiritual rituals, or simple recreation.

Archaeologists have even found evidence that farmers were cultivating *Cannabis sativa* and *Cannabis indica* as far back as 10000 BCE, making it one of the first true agricultural crops. Tobacco cultivation dates back almost as far in North and South America, while *Papaver somniferum*, also known as the "opium poppy," was being grown in parts of the Middle East as early as 3500 BCE.

Though a full history of drug and alcohol use would extend far beyond the scope of this book, it's not hard to appreciate that drug and alcohol use has transformed human culture far more than virtually anyone realizes.

8. Is there really such a thing as a gateway drug?

Beginning in the 1930s, one of the main rationales for cracking down on marijuana and hashish was what many researchers referred to as the Stepping-Stone Theory of Drug Abuse. According to this theory, using mild drugs such as cannabis *inevitably* led to more severe drug abuse, as well as addiction to narcotics. Since convicted heroin or cocaine addicts often reported having used cannabis at some point, antidrug campaigners demanded that cannabis use be brought under control due to its "corrupting influence." As a result, lawmakers in many jurisdictions established harsh penalties for anyone caught selling cannabis (or even using the drug) since that was seen as the only way to protect society from its influence.

Though the Stepping-Stone Theory has long since been disproven, it never went away completely. Even to this day, harsh penalties for cannabis use continue to be demanded by many courts, largely because cannabis is seen to be as dangerous as other, more addictive drugs.

As an alternative to the Stepping-Stone Theory, researchers during the 1970s proposed what would eventually be called the gateway hypothesis. According to this hypothesis, certain psychoactive substances such as cannabis and tobacco can increase the likelihood of other, more dangerous drugs being used in future. As opposed to the Stepping-Stone Theory that considered cannabis use as an inevitable first step to harder drugs, supporters of the gateway hypothesis argue that this isn't always the case.

Many young people who try cannabis, tobacco, or alcohol often stop at this stage without moving on to anything more severe. On the other hand, it is relatively rare for users to begin using hard drugs without beginning with "softer" drugs first. Gateway hypothesis supporters also acknowledge different risk factors that might influence users to move from legal to illegal drugs. These factors can include genetics, early childhood abuse, and peer pressure, and many of them will be discussed in Question 10.

Also, while cannabis is often considered to be the most important gateway drug, it isn't the only one. Tobacco and alcohol have also been suggested as possible gateway drugs since many chronic drug users begin their careers through drinking or smoking before moving on to more serious abuse. Even the recent popularity of e-cigarettes has raised concerns about whether adolescents and young people using them are more likely to progress to regular cigarette use or not (the latest research results suggest that it does).

But what is the current status of the gateway hypothesis? And should parents and teachers crack down on "lighter" drugs such as cannabis out of fear of what it could mean for young people becoming more serious abusers later on? A 2003 research study by the Drug Policy Research Center examined drug use patterns in more than 58,000 U.S. residents between the ages of 12 and 25 who took part in a nationwide study of substance abuse. While research results didn't rule out the gateway hypothesis completely, it did show that drug use can be influenced by a wide range of different factors, including family influence, genetics, and upbringing. What this means is that people can begin using drugs for many reasons, and fears about marijuana being a gateway drug seem largely exaggerated.

Still, while some of the milder psychoactive drugs such as marijuana or tobacco aren't necessarily gateway drugs, that doesn't necessarily mean they are harmless either. As we have already seen in Questions 1 and 2, drug dependence can form in many different ways, and any psychoactive substance is potentially addictive.

9. Is there a substance abuse epidemic?

As we have seen in Question 6, drug and alcohol abuse can be linked to millions of deaths worldwide, and the financial costs alone amount to many billions of dollars. But is this a problem that is getting worse with time? And what is the best way of determining that? Despite the difficulty in answering these questions, here are a few statistics to consider.

In looking at overdose deaths, for example, recent findings from the Centers for Disease Control and Prevention show the annual number of U.S. drug overdose deaths involving opioids (including prescription pain medications and heroin) has quadrupled since 1999. For 2015 alone, there were over 50,000 overdose deaths, up 11 percent from the previous year. Over that same period of time, deaths from heroin use alone rose 23 percent to 12,989 deaths in 2015.

When looking at other opioids, the death toll seems even more appalling. Overdose deaths involving the synthetic opioid fentanyl rose 73 percent to 9,580, while more well-known opioids such as OxyContin and Vicodin showed only a modest increase of 4 percent (but still accounting for 17,536 deaths). In Canada, the number of deaths linked to fentanyl and other opioids has also skyrocketed in recent years despite efforts to control its import from source countries such as China.

But there are other prescription drugs that are also prone to abuse. For example, central nervous system depressants such as diazepam (Valium), alprazolam (Xanax), and phenobarbital are also increasingly popular due to their value as tranquilizers and the willingness of many medical doctors to prescribe them for patients.

Since these medications can also reduce inhibitions and increase confidence and, in larger doses, euphoria, they have also gained a reputation as recreational drugs and are often purchased illegally when they can't be obtained by prescription. Not surprisingly, the number of overdose deaths linked to central nervous system depressants has also been on the rise since the 1990s. In 2015 alone, there were more than 8,700 overdose deaths linked to misuse of these medications.

Stimulants such as methylphenidate (Ritalin) have also become popular as an alternative to amphetamines since frequent prescribing of these drugs for children makes them increasingly available to potential abusers. As for more traditional drugs such as cocaine and benzodiazepines, available data also shows sharp upward trends over time though many of the overdose deaths linked to these drugs involve opioids as well.

In looking at deaths from alcohol overdose alone, there are an estimated 2,200 deaths in the United States each year (about six deaths a day) though actual statistics are harder to find since alcohol-related deaths aren't followed as scrupulously as drug deaths are. One important exception to this deals with the role alcohol plays in automobile accidents. According to the Centers for Disease Control and Prevention statistics, nearly one-third of all traffic deaths that occurred in the United States in 2014 alone were due to alcohol-impaired crashes. This amounts to nearly 10,000 fatalities in 2014. While legal and illegal drugs have been linked to 16 percent of all traffic accidents, alcohol use continues to be the main source of traffic deaths.

As the number of overdose deaths linked to many illegal drugs, especially opioids, continues to rise, lawmakers and treatment professionals are often at odds over how to save lives and help users overcome their addiction. Though we will be discussing some of the more promising

approaches being used such as harm reduction, greater policing of prescription medication, safe injection sites, and naloxone distribution later
in this book, it is important to recognize that there are no easy solutions.
Parents, teachers, and health professionals need to be vigilant since this is
definitely a problem that won't go away.

Causes and Risk Factors

10. What makes some people so vulnerable to substance abuse?

There is no easy answer to this question for the simple reason that addiction is something that can happen to literally anybody, at any point in our life span, and for a wide variety of reasons. As you can see in the case studies provided in this book, there is no one pathway to addiction. Whether the substance use occurs because someone is trying to self-medicate to escape emotional distress, due to peer pressure because other people are telling them that substance use is "cool," due to overuse of pain medication when dealing with chronic pain, or simply as a way to have fun, the risk of addiction is always there.

With that said, there do seem to be some predisposing factors that may make some people more vulnerable to addiction than others. Some of these factors include the following:

- *Adolescence*—For young people who pass the age of puberty and enter the difficult teenage years, the pressure they face in trying to become adults can be immense. That many of those same young people also face the temptation that comes with reduced parental supervision and greater independence means that they have more access to drugs and alcohol than they ever did before. Some researchers have even suggested that adolescents are particularly vulnerable to the influence of psychoactive substances because their central nervous systems are still in the process of developing.

- *Cultural acceptance*—Attitudes about certain psychoactive substances have a way of changing over time as more people come to accept its use. Fifty years ago, most young Americans smoked tobacco and many began smoking as soon as they reached adolescence. As new information about health risks became available, the percentage of young people who smoke has dropped to around 20 percent. In the same way, the popularity of new "party drugs" often depends on word of mouth and, more recently, on online information sources.

- *Biological predisposition to certain drugs*—Whether due to genetics or biochemical imbalances, some users may be unusually susceptible to drug or alcohol addiction. According to studies looking at the disease model of addiction, people with a family history of drug or alcohol abuse are prone to become addicted themselves. In fact, studies looking at identical twins suggest that different types of addictions have a 50–60 percent heritability. Heredity isn't destiny however, and many abusers are successful in overcoming addiction despite their family history.

- *Mental health issues*—People who develop serious mental health problems such as chronic depression, anxiety, or psychosis may often try to deal with their symptoms by "medicating" the problems away. This can also include people dealing with chronic pain who find life unbearable unless they continue taking pain medications, whether legally or illegally. Unfortunately, many people who rely on psychoactive substances to manage stress or emotional problems may find themselves unable to cope effectively without relying on substance use. And thus, a vicious circle begins.

- *Sensation-seeking*—According to psychologist Marvin Zuckerman, sensation-seeking is a personality trait that determines whether people are open to new and exciting experiences as well as willing to take risks. People high in this trait are prone to participating in activities such as "thrill-seeking," extreme sports, or illegal activities such as gambling or shoplifting. High sensation-seekers are also more likely to abuse stimulants, hallucinogens, or alcohol due to the "high" such drugs can bring and can quickly become dependent on them.

Not all risk factors can be easily identified, and many people may not even be aware that they are vulnerable. We will explore some more potential risk factors later in this book.

11. Is substance abuse linked to trauma?

All too frequently, people dealing with drug or alcohol addiction will also report a history of trauma, whether occurring in childhood or later in life. Though trauma can strike at any age, people who are traumatized as children are often most vulnerable.

Childhood trauma can take many forms, including physical or sexual abuse, sudden loss of one or both parents, being a witness to domestic violence, or dealing with parents who are substances abusers themselves. Still, the psychological impact of such trauma can last a lifetime since children may find themselves unable to form a normal sense of identity or basic control. They can also lose the chance to develop the natural resilience to stress that most of us take for granted.

There are a whole range of psychiatric diagnoses that can be applied to people dealing with the effects of long-term trauma. These include post-traumatic stress disorder, acute stress disorder, continuous traumatic stress disorder, and complex posttraumatic stress disorder though the underlying symptoms are often very similar.

Not only do trauma survivors tend to be hypervigilant (acutely sensitive to potential threats in their environment), but they often avoid any active emotional involvement with other people out of fear of being re-traumatized. Also, they may find themselves experiencing flashbacks whenever they are presented with situational triggers that remind them of past traumatic events.

While people dealing with childhood trauma can be successfully treated if they get help early enough, many survivors may prefer to hide what they are going through. They can also find themselves relying on unhealthy coping strategies to deal with trauma symptoms. Along with greater social isolation or relying on self-harm strategies to control stress (i.e., self-cutting or burning), trauma survivors are much more likely to abuse drugs and alcohol as a way of self-medicating their symptoms.

As you may expect, there are decades of research studies linking trauma (particularly childhood trauma) with later substance abuse though many addicts may prefer to hide their trauma history due to shame or guilt. Interestingly enough, new research studies have also shown a strong link between childhood trauma and non-substance-related forms of addiction (including gambling addiction and Internet addiction).

Until recently, treatment programs to help substance abusers with a history of trauma have been relatively rare. Many therapists working with addicts often focused on treating the substance abuse problem first and deferred treatment for issues stemming from abuse, along with other mental health problems, until later in the treatment process. This also meant leaving trauma symptoms untreated for much longer than really necessary. Also, since there were often no joint treatment programs available, addicts dealing with trauma typically find themselves attending different programs to deal with these problems separately.

Fortunately, more communities have recognized the need to provide integrated treatment to address problems such as substance abuse and trauma in a single program. Not only has research shown this combined approach works better than treating substance and trauma as separate disorders but is also much more cost efficient. More on this is discussed in the section on treatment and prevention.

12. What makes age of first drug or alcohol use so important?

Though substance abusers are most likely to begin abusing drugs or alcohol during their later teen years (16 or older), it's hardly uncommon for substance abuse to begin much earlier. One recent study following 1,420 children aged 9–16 years showed that children exposed to alcohol or other psychoactive substances before the age of 13 were at a substantial risk for developing a full-blown substance abuse disorder by the time they turned 16. This increased risk appears to decline in children aged 14 years or older though they showed the same level of risk as adolescents who began using substances later on.

Research looking at early exposure to drugs or alcohol has also found that children with behavior and emotional problems are particularly likely to develop later substance abuse problems. In that same study, boys, but not girls, dealing with depression appeared to be at increased risk for developing later issues with addiction. Behavior or conduct problems such as stealing, physical or emotional bullying, frequent truancy from school, and impulsive acting out (i.e., tantrums) were also linked to later substance abuse issues, particularly in children who developed these problems early in childhood, often in conjunction with other emotional issues.

Adolescents and preadolescents showing a repeated pattern of behavior problems are usually given the psychiatric diagnosis of conduct disorder, and chronic substance use is one of the main symptoms linked to this disorder. The two main forms of conduct disorders are *childhood-onset* conduct disorder, with conduct disorder symptoms developing before the

age of 10 years, and *adolescent-onset* conduct disorder, with behavior problems developing at a later age.

Not only is childhood-onset conduct disorder more likely to be associated with severe drug and/or alcohol abuse, but young people given this
diagnosis are also more likely to report a history of childhood physical
and sexual abuse. Other problems linked to early-onset conduct problems include early exposure to additional forms of trauma as well as being
neglected by their parents. They are also more likely to be exposed to substance use by their parents or older siblings, which can make them more
inclined to try drugs or alcohol for themselves.

As you might expect, the long-term consequences of childhood-onset
conduct problems can be severe. Not only are young offenders with a history of childhood-onset conduct problems more likely to become chronic
offenders even as adults, but they are also much more prone to impulsive
acting-out behavior, including violence.

For substance abusers seeking treatment, how successful that treatment
is often depends on the severity of the substance abuse problems. It also
means that people who begin abusing drugs/alcohol at an early age will
be much harder to treat given the length of time that they have been
abusing, not to mention the greater likelihood of health risks linked to
substance use. This is why treatment programs for adolescent substance
abusers are often of critical importance in helping to overcome addiction as well as preventing the severe consequences of letting this abuse
go untreated.

13. What about prenatal drug or alcohol exposure?

When considering the impact of early exposure to drugs or alcohol, it's
also important to look at how *prenatal* exposure can affect later development in children. The impact of prenatal alcohol exposure is particularly
important given the often tragic consequences that can follow. In its most
severe form, this is known as fetal alcohol syndrome, which can be identified by many of the following signs:

- An undersized head along with facial and cranial deformities
- Below-average height or weight
- Hyperactivity
- Cognitive impairments, including learning problems, poor judgment,
  and coordination

- Deformed limbs or fingers
- Vision or hearing problems
- Mood swings
- Poor social skills

In a less-severe form, children can have only a few of these signs without many of the obvious physical deformities. This is typically known as fetal alcohol exposure, and the two syndromes are usually classified together as fetal alcohol spectrum disorder (FASD). Along with birth defects, prenatal alcohol exposure can lead to premature births, which can also have long-term consequences for later development.

While the amount of alcohol that can be safely consumed during pregnancy remains controversial, FASD has been estimated to affect between 2 and 5 percent of all people in the United States and Europe alone. It is perhaps not surprising that the number of people with FASD is especially concentrated in the prison and mental health systems given their problems with impulsive acting-out behavior and substance abuse.

Although there are treatment programs available to help FASD children, the only way that it can be prevented is by avoiding alcohol when pregnant or when trying to get pregnant. Unfortunately, this can be a challenge given that surveys from the United States alone show that about 20–30 percent of women consume alcohol at some point in their pregnancies. In all, about 4.7 percent of expectant mothers are addicted to alcohol and often need medical help to control their drinking until their babies are safely delivered.

But there are other drugs that also have a potentially harmful effect during pregnancy. Though the greatest risk of birth defects can occur in the early stages of pregnancy (i.e., the first trimester), drug exposure can influence later development as well. While the effect these drugs have often varies depending on the type of drug used and the amount taken, certain drugs have been identified as having particularly strong prenatal effects. They include the following:

- Cocaine
- Heroin
- Marijuana
- MDMA
- Nicotine
- Methamphetamine
- Inhalants

There are also numerous prescription medications that can have a severe effect on fetal development. It is for this reason that pregnant women, or even women trying to get pregnant, should get medical advice about any medication they are taking.

Another risk associated with prenatal exposure to many psychoactive substances involves giving birth to infants with severe drug dependencies. One specific syndrome that has generated considerable concern in recent years is *neonatal opiate analgesic dependence* stemming from prenatal exposure to opioids. Along with birth complications, infants born opioid dependent often show problems such as diarrhea, irritability, sneezing, tremors, and chronic vomiting.

For pregnant women dealing with opioid addiction, the usual treatment involves placing them on methadone treatment to help wean them off other, potentially more dangerous, drugs (see next question). To reduce opiate dependency, pregnant women receiving methadone usually begin tapering off their dosage in the weeks leading up to delivery. While the infants will still be born dependent on methadone, detox is relatively straightforward and shouldn't lead to later complications if other issues such as poor nutrition can be avoided.

As for drugs such as cocaine, the available evidence suggests that newborn infants dealing with prenatal exposure often experience problems with irritability, insomnia, hyper-alertness, and a poor feeding response. Even though the effects of cocaine withdrawal in infants don't appear to be as severe as with opioids or alcohol, research has shown evidence of significant long-term problems with language, cognitive functioning, and behavior.

Treatment programs for pregnant women dealing with substance abuse also focus on many of the other problems that can lead to later health problems for their infants. Not only are many pregnant women likely to be addicted to more than one drug, including alcohol and opioids, but they often face issues such as poor nutrition for potential infection from unsafe needle use. Through therapy and careful monitoring of their health during and after pregnancy, many of the problems associated with prenatal substance use can be reduced, if not eliminated altogether. This helps ensure that their children will have an improved chance for a normal life.

14. Why are opioids so addictive?

To see how opioids can have such a powerful effect, it is important to understand the way in which the human body deals with pain. Though pain can occur for a variety of reasons, including physical damage to the body or inflammation, we become aware that we are in pain only when neural pathways known as *nociceptors* are activated. Once activated, these pathways then relay information about pain to key regions of the brain such as the thalamus and the cerebral cortex. It is then that the body responds to this sensation of pain by releasing specialized hormones called *endorphins*, which are produced in the central nervous system and the pituitary gland.

There are different classes of endorphins such as alpha-endorphins, beta-endorphins, and gamma-endorphins though they all share a chemical structure very similar to morphine or heroin. To help endorphins counteract pain, our bodies have specialized opiate receptors which then block pain signals. Endorphins can also be produced by stress and fear and appear to be part of the body's natural "fight or flight" response.

Once the brain begins producing endorphins in large quantities, this increased activation of our opiate receptors produces a sensation of euphoria not unlike the drug high produced by heroin or morphine. This is why many athletes report feeling euphoria after a strenuous workout, something that has been borne out by brain imaging research. In the same way, laughter or other strong positive emotions can stimulate endorphin production and also lead to euphoria. In fact, a 2011 study showed that people attending a comedy club have a reduced sensitivity to pain due to higher endorphin production.

As you can see, we have been designed by evolution to have extremely sensitive opiate receptors in the brain and the central nervous system. Since opioids such as heroin, morphine, and fentanyl act on the brain's opiate receptors in the same way that natural endorphins do, this makes us especially vulnerable to opioid addiction.

At this time, one of the most well-known treatments for combating opioid dependency involves the use of methadone maintenance treatment. First developed in the 1930s, methadone is widely used around the world as a pain medication as well as for anesthesia. While methadone has the same risks of drug dependence existence as for opioids such as heroin and morphine, it is highly effective in helping addicts overcome cravings as well as blocking the euphoria that other drugs can produce. Also, methadone detoxification is relatively fast making it an ideal treatment for opioid addicts seeking to get off drugs altogether. Since methadone can also be abused as a street drug, access is tightly controlled in most jurisdictions, and medical doctors can prescribe it only after completing a specialized training program. Despite its effectiveness, methadone maintenance treatment remains controversial, with many social activists suggesting that it can do more harm than good.

Another effective treatment involves the use of opioid antagonists such as naloxone and naltrexone. Naloxone (sold under the brand name of Narcan) bonds to opioid receptors in the central nervous system allowing it to counteract the effects of most opioids rapidly. For this reason, it has become a standard treatment for all forms of opioid overdoses as well as reducing depression and respiratory problems.

Since naloxone is legal just about everywhere with a prescription, many states and provinces have authorized the distributing of naloxone "kits" to medical clinics and hospital emergency rooms. Ambulances are also including these kits as standard equipment so that paramedics can administer naloxone injections to any patient dealing with an opioid overdose. In fact, countries such as Australia and Canada are making naloxone kits available at pharmacies and even as "take-home" kits for substance abusers to use when dealing with an accidental overdose.

15. Can peer pressure lead to substance abuse?

For people of all ages, peer pressure can have a powerful impact on the choices they make, but it can be especially dangerous for adolescents and young adults. For adolescents especially, the need for approval from the people around them, especially people their own age, can be an important part of developing good self-esteem. This peer pressure can often be seen in the way young people talk, dress, and act and also in the kind of values they may embrace, something their parents may find hard to accept.

While peer pressure can certainly be positive, including learning to be more independent and embracing positive behaviors such as participating in sports or other extracurricular activities, it can lead to riskier behavior as well. One of the most well-documented findings in social psychology is the *risky-shift effect*, or the tendency for people to be more likely to make risky decisions when they are part of a group than they would by themselves. In other words, people are much more likely to engage in risky behavior such as unsafe sex or substance use when they are surrounded by other people willing to do the same.

For adolescents and young adults in particular, being around other people their age who are willing to drink or use drugs can be a powerful lure to trying the same thing themselves. Not only does seeing other people breaking these social taboos make them more likely to do the same, but many of these same peers can also act as a support group to help deal with any negative consequences afterward.

Another factor that seems closely linked to the role that peer pressure can play in risk behavior deals with *social capital*, or the quality of the social networks on which people depend. This is usually measured in terms of the extent to which people feel that they are part of a larger community of friends, acquaintances, and family members who can provide emotional support when needed. Though this can often change as we grow older, adolescents seem particularly vulnerable to developing substance abuse problems due to a lack of strong social bonds with friends and family. Not only do strong family ties help protect young people from substance abuse, but they are also important in helping addicts overcome substance abuse problems. This can also help explain why young people who are made to feel like "outsiders" are often more vulnerable to the kind of influences that can lead to substance abuse.

As we grow older, the impact of peer pressure becomes less of an issue in shaping how we behave though its influence never goes away completely. Even as adults, our friendship networks can play a role in the lifestyle choices we make, including whether or not we decide to use substances such as tobacco and alcohol or other psychoactive substances. For people trying to overcome drug or alcohol addiction, being surrounded by friends or acquaintances who are users themselves can often sabotage any attempt at getting clean. It is for this reason that substance abuse treatment programs often focus on establishing support networks that can help addicts avoid these negative peer influences. For adolescent substance abusers in particular, having family members or friends taking take part in the treatment process can often be an important part of the recovery process.

16. Is there such a thing as an addictive personality?

While we have seen in Question 10 that people may be especially vulnerable to drug or alcohol addiction due to genetic history, emotional problems, physical or sexual abuse, or early childhood trauma, the common belief that certain personality traits can lead to addiction is largely a myth and a dangerous one. Also known as the *psychogenic*, or character defect theory of addiction, this theory laid the blame for addiction on the addicts' inability to control their own innate impulses, leading to drug or alcohol addiction.

Much of the early research that attempted to prove a link between personality and addiction largely focused on such traits as risk-seeking, sensation-seeking, and impulsiveness. Extraversion is another trait that was often found in drug and alcohol abusers, leading some psychologists to argue that these stable personality traits may be causing people to become addicted to psychoactive substances, not to mention various addictive behaviors such as problem gambling, smoking, unsafe sex, or dangerous "thrill-seeking."

And then there is *psychopathy*, which is typically characterized by impaired empathy, egotistical thinking and behavior, and impulsive acting-out behavior. While substance abuse has long been linked to personality diagnoses such as psychopathy and antisocial personality disorder, this is largely due to the widespread use of drugs and alcohol among people convicted of criminal offenses. Part of the problem with this kind of research is that, considering drugs are illegal in most jurisdictions, drug abusers are often classified as criminals even if they have never committed any other offenses.

As you can see, people who abuse drugs or alcohol may well score highly on many personality inventories measuring these specific traits. As a result, inappropriate use of these personality measures often led to people being misidentified as being "doomed" to become addicts, or, at the very least, to be at a high risk for potential addiction and, in some cases, to act as a self-fulfilling prophecy.

More recently however, researchers have taken a closer look at many of the studies that were used to prove the link between personality and addiction and the problems many of these studies have. Since most of these early studies looked at people who were *already* substance abusers, there is no way to tell whether these key personality traits were causing the addiction or whether they were a consequence of addiction. Perhaps more important, none of these studies showed that personality testing could be used to prevent substance abuse from occurring in the first place.

While there is no such thing as an addictive personality, it is important to recognize that people can be vulnerable to drug or alcohol addiction for many different reasons, some of which have already been explored in Question 10. And that can include personality traits such as high sensation-seeking or risk-taking, which can lead people to experiment with mind-altering substances. Though this experimenting doesn't always lead progresses to a full-blown addiction, it is still important to recognize that risk-taking behavior can have serious consequences that far too many people may ignore until too late.

17. Is substance abuse linked to poor parenting?

Many parents who discover that their child is an addict may well wonder if they were responsible somehow. This ties into the common misconception that only "bad parents" can have children who are addicts. On the other hand, it's hardly uncommon to find substance abusers who report dealing with various family problems that might have played a role in their abuse. These problems can include having a parent who abuses drugs or alcohol, being exposed to domestic violence, experiencing emotional neglect, or dealing with early traumatic experiences such as physical or sexual abuse.

Research looking at parenting and how it can lead to problem behaviors such as substance abuse typically focuses on *negative parenting* (emotional neglect, lack of positive reinforcement, failing to set proper limits, poor monitoring) as being most likely to lead to later problems. Also, young people growing up with an alcohol- or drug-abusing parent can often find themselves at risk for developing addiction problems themselves due to the genetic risk as well as the adverse environment in which they are raised. It is for this reason that many treatment programs specifically target children of addicts to prevent them from becoming addicted themselves.

On the other hand, positive parenting, including emotional closeness between parents and their children as well as close monitoring and a supportive parenting style, is generally seen to protect children from many of the influences that might lead to substance abuse. Other positive parenting strategies include rule-setting (along with clear consequences when those rules are broken), praise, and physical affection, as well as amount of quality time spent with children and maintaining good communication.

Unfortunately, there are limits to how effective these positive strategies can be as children grow older and they form social networks with other adolescents. Counteracting the effect of peer pressure and adverse influences such as bullying can be close to impossible for many parents who are often caught by surprise in learning that their children have become secretive about their activities away from home.

In much the same way that positive parenting can help protect children from substance abuse, it can play a critical role in helping substance abusers seek help and learn to overcome addiction. While parents often need time to come to terms with learning that their child has a drug or alcohol problem, how they respond to this revelation, whether it is something a child has confessed directly or learned about after their child is hospitalized, is something that needs to be carefully considered.

Though many parents may choose to deny that a child of theirs could be an addict or else react with anger, someone coming to terms with being an addict often needs parental love and support more than anything else. Accepting that their children need help and encouraging them to seek out this help is just the first step however. For this reason, many treatment professionals prefer to work directly with parents and other family members to help them understand more about substance abuse as well as making them part of the treatment process. Not only can this make overcoming addiction easier, but it can also help bring parents and their children closer together.

18. Is substance abuse genetic?

While the nature versus nurture argument is probably as old as psychology itself, findings from decades of research have shown a strong genetic influence for nicotine use, alcoholism, and use of illegal substances. Until recently, most of these research studies have focused on family and twin studies examining risk of substance abuse in people with a shared genetic history.

One of the most comprehensive of these studies, the Minnesota Twin Family Study (MTFS), is a long-term project looking at 1,400 pairs of twins who, along with their parents, were assessed at regular intervals beginning at age 11 and continuing well into adulthood. Along with psychological testing, the MTFS twins underwent brain imaging, and data on substance use at different ages, along with parental substance use, was also collected. In looking at age of first drink, the correlation between identical twin pairs was significantly higher than fraternal twin pairs for both boys and girls. Since identical twins essentially share the same genes while fraternal twins are no more similar than regular siblings, this finding is consistent with numerous other studies showing a strong genetic component for substance abuse.

In recent years, researchers have identified specific gene markers, which appear strongly linked to the likelihood of developing different forms of substance abuse. For example, the CHRM2 gene, which is an acetylcholine receptor associated with key brain functions, has been implicated in family studies of alcoholics along with other traits such as sensation-seeking, novelty-seeking, and antisocial behavior. Another gene marker, DRD4 located on chromosome 11 has also been linked to substance abuse, along with antisocial behavior, impulsivity, and sensation-seeking. Other studies have identified specific gene regions on chromosome 1, 2, 7, and 10, which appear linked to alcohol dependence and childhood conduct disorder and attention deficit hyperactivity disorder. Still, it is important to note that none of these studies have identified a gene marker that is specifically linked to substance abuse as opposed to other personality traits and behaviors that are usually linked with drug or alcohol addiction.

As it stands, does having these gene markers mean that someone is "doomed" to become an addict? While there is evidence of a strong genetic component to addiction, that is, behavioral genetics, how genetic factors can influence behavioral choices can be difficult to predict considering that environment can have just as important a role. Even individuals with a close family history of addiction will not necessarily become addicts as well due to the conscious choices they will make in life. For that matter, someone without a genetic history of substance abuse may still become an addict due to childhood abuse, mental health issues, or other environmental influences.

Genetic research is still valuable in identifying individuals who may be at an increased risk for drug or alcohol addiction and, as a result, may need early intervention to prevent problems from developing later in life. This includes providing genetic counseling for adolescents or young adults with a family history of drug or alcohol abuse and advising them of potential risks that, with proper guidance, can be avoided completely.

19. Are sexual minorities more vulnerable to substance abuse?

Over the past few decades, research studies have consistently shown much higher drug and alcohol use in men and women belonging to sexual minorities than in their heterosexual counterparts. According to one recent meta-analysis looking at sexual minority adolescents, the odds of reporting different forms of substance abuse can be three times what can be observed in heterosexual adolescents. Along with other negative psychosocial consequences such as suicide and depression, homosexual, bisexual, and transgender men and women remain strongly at risk for drug and alcohol abuse, something that needs to be considered when seeking treatment.

To understand why sexual minorities are so vulnerable to substance abuse and other mental health problems, it is important to understand what researchers have termed "minority stress theory." According to this theory, sexual minorities experience unique stress issues stemming from the active discrimination and harassment they frequently face. Despite greater acceptance in recent years, this stress can range from legal discrimination in many jurisdictions to the more personal harassment they can experience from friends and family. In addition, there is internalized self-hatred to deal with, especially in individuals who have been raised to see same-sex sexual attraction as evil or disgusting.

Considering the emotional issues that can arise from this kind of stress, it is hardly surprising that substance use has become so common as a coping mechanism for many individuals who may feel overwhelmed in their search for acceptance. Also, many people in the process of "coming out" may seek companionship through the "bar scene" where they may often be exposed to alcohol and other addictive substances, but they may also face pressures that they might not be ready for in the hope of becoming accepted.

Recent research looking at different sources of stress faced by homosexual, bisexual, and transgender men and women also suggests that the link between minority stress and substance abuse may be much more complicated than was previously believed. For example, sexual minority group members reporting a recent history of being victimized, that is, verbally or physically assaulted, appear much more likely to use cannabis to cope with stress than non-victims. While other drugs may be used as well, cannabis appears to be the most popular. When looking at stress due to internalized stigma (having negative attitudes about same-sex relations), alcohol use appears to be the most popular method of coping, with other drugs being less likely to be used. In general, however, study results consistently show members of sexual minorities primarily use drugs or alcohol to cope with minority stress rather than for enjoyment.

Unfortunately, being a member of a sexual minority can make it extremely difficult for many people to admit having a substance abuse problem and seeking treatment. Along with issues surrounding the coming-out process, finding a gay- or transgender-friendly counselor or program can be much harder in some places than others. Seeking treatment can also be complicated by the type of relationship sexual minority group members have with their families and whether they can get the emotional support that heterosexual substance abusers often take for granted. The Directory of Resources lists some organizations that can help, and other links can be found online or with the help of local health agencies.

20. Are military veterans coping with trauma more likely to become substance abusers?

It's hard to say how prevalent drug abuse really is in the military considering veterans caught abusing drugs are often prosecuted and, if convicted, can receive a dishonorable discharge. Due to the zero tolerance policies currently in place in the U.S. military, actual incidence of drug abuse remains far lower than in the general population.

On the other hand, alcohol and tobacco abuse among men and women in military service remains far higher than in the general population. According to statistics provided by the U.S. Department of Defense, 47 percent of all active duty services members reported engaging in binge drinking in 2008—up from 35 percent in 1998. Around 20 percent of military personnel on active duty reported binge drinking every week in the previous month—and this is far higher for military personnel with high combat exposure.

As for tobacco use, only 30 percent of service members reported being smokers, which is roughly equivalent to tobacco use in civilians though, again, tobacco use is far higher in military personnel who have been in combat.

When looking at veterans who have mustered out of the military, the prevalence of drug and alcohol problems is rapidly reaching epidemic proportions—especially for veterans who have served in active combat overseas. In a recent study of returning veterans who have participated in Operations Enduring Freedom, Iraqi Freedom, and New Dawn (OEF/OIF/OND) and were seeking treatment, 76.2 percent were diagnosed with a substance abuse disorder. No real difference was found between male and female veterans.

Veterans dealing with substance abuse often struggle with additional mental health problems, of which the most common is posttraumatic stress disorder (PTSD). Among U.S. veterans, the lifetime prevalence of PTSD ranges from 6.2 to 18.7 percent, and for veterans who have served in active military operations overseas, the incidence of posttraumatic stress symptoms is often much higher. Many veterans dealing with trauma may turn to alcohol or other psychoactive substances as a form of self-medication to deal with flashbacks, hypervigilance, and other symptoms linked to trauma. Related mental health problems such as depression, anxiety, and diminished overall quality of life can also contribute to substance abuse.

For veterans who have been injured while deployed overseas, chronic pain is also a serious concern. Among U.S. veterans alone, an estimated 28 percent of health-care patients report moderate to severe pain as they cope with traumatic amputations, head injuries, or other serious injuries that might have been fatal in previous conflicts. For this reason, abuse of pain medication prescriptions (particularly opioid medications) is a growing problem among current and former members of the military. These medications can be either prescribed by military doctors or, in other cases, purchased illegally to help with severe pain.

Though many veterans may be reluctant to admit to needing help for PTSD or substance abuse, Veterans' Administration (VA) treatment programs are available in most major metropolitan areas. Veterans and family members needing help can contact their local VA medical center or health-care provider. Information on the VA's general information hotline and online resources can be found in the Directory of Resources.

❖

Consequences of Substance Abuse

21. How quickly can someone become addicted to drugs or alcohol?

As we have already seen in Question 10, not everyone is going to react to drugs or alcohol in exactly the same way and not everyone is going to become an addict. Whether due to genetics, upbringing, emotional issues, or personality differences, some people are going to be more vulnerable to psychological or physiological dependence than other people who try drugs or alcohol. And there is no way of reliably predicting who is going to become an addict and who isn't.

People may start taking drugs or alcohol due to curiosity, a need to seem "cool" to others, or as a way of escaping emotional or physical pain. Still, the main reason they will keep taking drugs afterward is the pleasurable sensations that many psychoactive substances can produce. While nobody is going to become addicted after only one or two times, the speed with which the central nervous system and other parts of the body adapt to these new chemicals can make drug tolerance occur much faster than users might expect. That means that users need to take even more of the drug to get the same sense of pleasure and, after a while, it also leads to withdrawal effects when regular doses of the drug are disrupted.

Another sign that addiction has developed is when certain "triggers" can increase the likelihood of using drugs or alcohol again. Whether it involves a stressful situation or interpersonal conflict that users need to escape from or for pleasure, users encountering these triggers soon learn to associate them with substance use. For example, many alcoholics describe themselves as "social drinkers" since they rarely drink alone and prefer to attend gatherings where alcohol is freely served and where everyone else drinks as well. This makes the social gathering into a trigger for drinking. On the other hand, someone who is dealing with trauma and experiencing flashbacks or other posttraumatic symptoms may rely on drugs or alcohol as a form of self-medication. This makes the flashbacks or other traumatic reminders into a trigger for substance use, which, in turn, makes the combined substance abuse/PTSD extremely difficult to treat.

The important point to remember is that this sense of dependence people develop for drugs or alcohol usually grows worse with time. Though many users may decide that they can deal with their substance dependence themselves rather than seeking treatment, this is much harder to accomplish than they might think. Through proper counseling, people with substance issues can learn to handle triggers that might otherwise sabotage their recovery. Also, the relapses that often occur can lead users to believe that they are untreatable, which may lead them into a downward spiral. This is why dealing with trained substance abuse counselors can be so important, especially for substance abusers in the very early stages. Recognizing and dealing with addiction before it has a chance to become a threat to physical health can be the best form of preventative medicine.

22. Are substance abusers at risk for suicide?

Based on numerous research studies, there seems little doubt that people with drug or alcohol problems face an increased risk for suicide. A 2004 meta-analytic study showed that individuals treated for substance abuse are 9 or 10 times more likely to commit suicide compared with the general population. Psychological autopsy studies examining suicide deaths indicate that drug or alcohol abuse represent one of the most common mental health problems reported, second only to mood disorders such as depression.

The link between alcohol abuse and suicide seems particularly strong, with alcoholics being 60–120 times more likely to attempt suicide than nonalcoholics. But other drugs, including cocaine and opiates, have been implicated as well. Results of coroners' inquests from 13 U.S.

states showed evidence of cocaine use in 9–17 percent of all suicides and opiate use in 8–18 percent of deaths depending on the racial/ethnic group. A 2005 Australian study found that approximately 16 percent of amphetamine-related deaths and 11 percent of opiate-related deaths were suicides. Overall, stimulants (including cocaine and amphetamines) and opiates seem most likely to be linked to suicide mortality though other drugs have been associated with suicide deaths as well.

In exploring risk factors that might increase the risk of substance-related suicides, researchers have focused on the following:

- *Severity of substance abuse*—People who begin abusing substances early or who have a history of polysubstance abuse seem particularly prone to eventual death from suicide. This often includes co-occurring use of multiple drugs, including alcohol, as well as starting drug or alcohol use at an early age.
- *Presence of other mental health issues*—This can include depression, anxiety, major mental illness, social inadequacy, and various personality disorders.
- *History of abuse, particularly childhood abuse*—People reporting a childhood history of physical, emotional, or sexual abuse seem especially vulnerable to suicide and substance use.
- *History of family adversity*—Even for people who may not report being abused directly, having a family history of adversity can increase the risk of suicide as well as addiction. This can include having parents who were substance abusers, unstable family environment, witnessing domestic abuse, or a family history of mental health problems.
- *Family history of suicide*—While there may be a genetic component to depression or other mental health problems linked to suicide, having a close family member who has taken his or her own life can greatly increase the risk that a substance user might commit suicide as well.
- *Active intoxication of drugs or alcohol*—For many substance abusers, the greatest risk is often while they are under the influence of drugs or alcohol when their inhibitions are greatly loosened and they are far more inclined to give in to suicidal impulses.
- *Type of drugs used*—Along with the generally increased risk of suicide in substance abusers, recent research suggests that people who abuse opioids, cocaine, or sedatives may be especially prone to engage in suicidal behaviors. Polysubstance abusers who combine drugs and alcohol are also at increased risk.
- *Violent behavior*—Research has shown that people who are physically violent while under the influence of drugs or alcohol are also prone to

committing suicide. Possible reasons include the increased tendency toward impulsive behavior seen in violent individuals, which can also lead to impulsive suicide attempts, as well as committing suicide out of fear that they might otherwise injure people close to them.

For anyone dealing with substance abuse, whether directly or in a close family member, the possibility of suicide is something that should always be considered. This is what makes early intervention and treatment so critical, especially if any of the risk factors listed are also present.

23. How does substance use affect the brain?

Different psychoactive substances can affect the brain and central nervous system in different ways. As you have seen in Question 14, opioids affect the brain by acting on the brain's natural opiate receptors and mimicking the effects of endorphins in controlling pain. This is what makes drugs such as heroin, morphine, and opium so potent as well as making them extremely addictive.

Alcohol, on the other hand, affects the brain by increasing the effect of inhibitory neurotransmitters, particularly gamma-aminobutyric acid. This leads to sluggish motor activity and slurred speech. Alcohol also inhibits the production of glutamate, an excitatory neurotransmitter which is critical in voluntary motor activity as well as mental functions such as learning and memory.

Because of the complicated role that alcohol can play in brain functioning, different regions of the brain can be affected in different ways. Alcohol's influence on the cerebral cortex results in a loss of behavior inhibition as well as slowing down the processing of sensory data from the various sense organs. It also inhibits the brain's ability to process information making thinking much more difficult. Alcohol also affects the cerebellum's ability to control movement and balance, leading to the "falling-down drunk" syndrome so often seen in people who are intoxicated. The effect of alcohol on other regions of the brain such as the medulla oblongata and the hypothalamus can lead to sleepiness and disruptions in the natural hormone production of the body.

Even a small amount of alcohol can lead to short-term blackouts, though the effects are usually temporary unless the amount of alcohol consumed becomes life threatening. But alcohol also acts as a diuretic causing the body to become extremely dehydrated. The process of metabolizing alcohol also forces the body to deplete its natural stores of thiamine (vitamin B1). This leads to the well-known hangover effect that drinkers often experience the following morning. Again, while hangovers are usually temporary, they can also be a warning of the damage that chronic alcoholism can cause to your body. Needless to say, the old adage about "the hair of the dog that bit you" doesn't apply, and drinking more alcohol does *not* eliminate a hangover.

Another drug that is well known for how it affects the brain is cocaine. Due to its powerful stimulant properties, cocaine boosts the brain's natural dopamine levels, leading to short-term hypersensitivity to light, sound, and touch as well as producing feelings of extreme happiness and energy. Since dopamine is a neurotransmitter that controls the brain's reward centers, it can play a strong role in addiction. Researchers have found that many drugs, including cocaine and heroin, will trigger a strong release of dopamine in the nucleus accumbens, a cluster of nerve cells in the basal forebrain linked to the hypothalamus. Long known as the brain "pleasure center," virtually any sensation of pleasure is linked to increased activity in this area of the brain. Basically, drug use acts as a shortcut to stimulating this pleasure center with dopamine, with the pleasurable memories associated with that drug use being laid down by the adjoining hypothalamus. In turn, this leads to the kind of conditioning that makes drug use into a habit that can be extremely hard to break.

As you can see, drugs and alcohol can have a wide range of different effects on the brain and the rest of the central nervous system depending on the type and amount that is taken. We will explore more about the short-term and long-term consequences of drug and alcohol use in Questions 25 and 26.

24. Do some drugs of abuse have medical benefits?

As we look back at the history of drug use, many of these drugs were initially introduced as potential treatments for different medical conditions. For example, heroin was originally marketed as a "nonaddictive" pain reliever that was safe to use for children and adults alike. In the same way, cocaine was first introduced as a way of helping morphine and opium addicts overcome addiction, something that quickly backfired.

Other drugs such as LSD (lysergic acid diethylamide) were used by researchers for decades to treat mental illness and alcoholism until being eventually banned. Also, prescription pain relievers such as fentanyl and OxyContin can have powerful benefits in treating chronic pain, though the potential for abuse cannot be underestimated. For that matter, researchers have been getting positive results using drugs such as MDMA (ecstasy) in treating severe posttraumatic stress disorder though, again, this research continues to be controversial.

In recent years, we have also seen marijuana being increasingly prescribed for medical purposes and, under proper conditions, can be effective in treating pain and discomfort from a wide range of medical conditions. Again though, the benefits of marijuana use need to be carefully balanced against the risk of potential abuse, something that many users may not fully consider. In recent years, many countries and even some U.S. states are now legalizing the sale and use of marijuana. As a result, we are likely to see how this growing trend toward liberalized marijuana laws plays out on a wider scale, especially since medical marijuana seems to be a useful alternative to more addictive pain relievers such as opioids.

Other countries also allow the medical use of proscribed drugs under controlled circumstances. In the United Kingdom, for example, diamorphine (heroin) can be prescribed by physicians who have a special dispensing license, much like how methadone is prescribed in North America. Usually used for treating chronic pain, heroin can be extremely effective, with the risk of addiction usually being no greater than that for other opiates. More important, methadone treatment is much more widely used than in the United States, so people who become addicted can be treated safely and effectively.

As for cocaine, medical use is allowed in countries such as Canada and Australia, usually for treating depression though this is carefully monitored to prevent the drug from being misused. Even in the United States, cocaine is available for use in hospitals and medical centers (mainly as a local anesthetic) though it continues to be covered under the Controlled Substances Act.

As you can see from these different examples, many of these normally illegal drugs can be used under strict medical supervision and only for treatment of certain medical conditions. At the same time, the risk of potential addiction is always present in much the same way as it is for many other prescription medications that need to be carefully monitored by medical doctors. Even with this monitoring however, many of these medications can still get diverted to be sold as street drugs such as fentanyl, OxyContin, and Ritalin. This is what makes using proscribed substances for medical purposes so dangerous. None of these drugs should be taken without careful consideration of the potential benefits and risks involved. Patients also need to be warned about the hazards of misusing these medications as well as what might happen if they are used by people for whom they haven't been prescribed.

25. What are some of the short-term consequences of substance abuse?

As we have already seen in Question 23, drugs and alcohol have a profound effect on the brain and central nervous system. While most psychoactive substances can cause euphoria and other pleasurable sensations in the short run, the potential dangers of even first-time use cannot be underestimated.

With alcohol, for example, how severe the impact can be for first-time users depends on the amount of alcohol consumed. Along with the risk of alcohol poisoning (which is potentially fatal), people consuming more alcohol than their body can safely handle may experience breathing difficulties, possible coma, uncontrolled urination and defecation, and vomiting. In moderate doses, alcohol can lead to lower body core temperature, slurred speech, altered emotion, blurred vision, and an increased need to urinate. Even mild alcohol consumption can lead to impaired judgment, slower reflexes, concentration problems, and poor reaction time. This is what makes driving while under the influence of alcohol so dangerous since the risk of accidents rises substantially, even for people who might not believe that alcohol use has affected their ability to drive. For this reason, many jurisdictions prosecute drivers under the age of 21 who have even low levels of alcohol in their system.

As for other drugs, the risks can also be severe given that overdosing may occur even in first-time users. With heroin, for example, short-term effects can include lethargy, reduced pain sensation, and heavy sensation in the arms and legs. Though heroin users often experience a pleasurable "rush" sensation, this passes quickly and, as their bodies adapt, they will need more and more of the drug to have the same sensation. This also boosts the risk of overdosing. Another danger with heroin use is the effect it can have on breathing, which becomes much slower, sometimes to the point of being life threatening. Many of the same problems associated with heroin can also be found in other opioids such as OxyContin and fentanyl. Given the sharp increase in opioid overdose deaths we have seen in recent years, potential users need to educate themselves about the serious risks involved with any kind of opioid use.

For cocaine users, the short-term effects can include a short-lived intense high that often passes quickly and is soon followed by a craving for more of the drug as well as withdrawal-type effects. Cocaine can produce increased heart rate, muscle spasms, convulsions, and emotional instability that users are often unprepared to handle. There is also an increased risk for cardiovascular problems (heart attack or stroke), seizures, or breathing failure depending on how much has been taken.

Another concern that needs to be raised is that very few drugs purchased on the street or from suspicious sources are actually "pure." That means that whoever is selling the drug often "cuts" them with another substance to increase its volume or to provide an extra "kick." According to drug enforcement agencies, drugs such as heroin can be anywhere from 5 to 99 percent pure.

In fact, some street drugs may have almost none of the drug that sellers purportedly claim is present. Some cutting agents can include artificial sweeteners, lactose, aspirin, ephedrine, or even other kinds of drugs such as methamphetamine or ketamine. This can make the potential effects of these unknown chemicals completely unpredictable, not to mention life threatening.

As you can see, even the short-term consequences of drug and alcohol use can be hard to determine given the potential impact these different substances can have on the human body, all of which makes overdose deaths so common, particularly when dealing with street drugs with unknown ingredients.

26. What are the long-term consequences of substance abuse?

There are a wide range of serious medical problems that have been linked to chronic drug or alcohol abuse. Leaving aside the dangers of sharing unsterilized needles, drug overdosing, or using street drugs that have been adulterated with other substances that can make them more lethal, long-term substance use involves additional hazards that need to be better understood by most users.

With alcohol, for example, there is some controversy over whether moderate alcohol use can help prevent certain medical problems though, again, this doesn't apply to chronic alcohol use. Long-term alcohol abusers, on the other hand, often experience liver damage, especially cirrhosis of the liver, cardiovascular disease, anemia, and an increased risk of stroke.

Chronic alcohol use can also damage the brain and central nervous system in different ways. Along with creating numerous brain lesions and altering the brain's biochemistry, alcoholics often suffer from nutritional problems that can lead to severe complications as well.

One of the most devastating examples of this is the condition known as Wernicke-Korsakoff syndrome. This syndrome is most often seen in chronic alcoholics, who, due to poor health habits and alcohol use, develop a severe deficiency of vitamin B1 in their diet. In the short run, lack of vitamin B1 can lead to a condition known as Wernicke's encephalopathy, in which bleeding in the brain's limbic system leads to mental confusion, unsteady gait, and visual problems. Though emergency treatment, including vitamin supplements, can help with the symptoms, episodes of Wernicke's encephalopathy typically lead to more long-term problems, including chronic Korsakoff psychosis.

Even after the Wernicke symptoms subside, people who progress to full-blown Korsakoff syndrome develop severe memory problems, including the inability to form new memories as well as loss of many of their previous memories. They can also experience hallucinations and language and other cognitive problems. Korsakoff patients often require long-term care since there is no known treatment.

There are other forms of dementia relating to chronic alcohol use, including alcohol-related dementia, though they are often harder to diagnose since the symptoms for these different conditions tend to be so similar. Also, given that chronic alcoholism can lead to problems with cardiovascular events or head injury, people with drinking problems may be prone to Alzheimer's disease or similar disorders. Though alcoholic dementia can be successfully treated if caught early enough, most of these other conditions tend to be permanent.

As for medical problems resulting from other kinds of drug use, that can be harder to determine though there is no disputing that users are prone to related problems such as exposure to infectious diseases (including HIV and hepatitis A though G) along with other chronic illnesses. Still, looking at specific drugs can provide some idea of the kind of long-term health problems that can occur.

With opioids such as heroin, for example, evidence indicates that long-term use can affect the reward system of the brain and central nervous system, leading to chronic dependence. In addition, autopsy studies of the brains of opioid addicts show indications of significant brain inflammation and the buildup of proteins, which can produce a syndrome that resembles Alzheimer's disease in many ways. Many researchers argue that chronic opioid abuse can lead to *premature aging* of the brain, including the development of symptoms that are more commonly seen in patients who are much older. It remains unclear whether this kind of damage is reversible, but a detox program accompanied by proper medical supervision can help opioid addicts learn to manage their symptoms.

While other drugs such as cocaine, LSD, gamma-hydroxybutyrate (GHB), methamphetamine, tobacco, and ketamine are also known to produce neurological effects, at least in the short run, there still aren't that may studies looking at long-term health problems. Still, given the psychological and physiological effects of euphoria-inducing substances, it's hardly surprising that chronic substance abusers are especially vulnerable to a wide range of medical conditions, not to mention drastically shortened lifespans.

27. How does substance abuse affect families?

There are few things more devastating to most families than dealing with a family member who has a drug or alcohol addiction. Given that virtually every addict has at least one or more family members who are directly affected by this abuse, it is safe to say that the psychological consequences of living in this kind of environment can often be just as damaging as what the addict is going through. Whether this involves dealing with a drug or alcohol abusing child, spouse, or parent, the number of family members directly affected by abuse is typically far greater than the substance abusers themselves.

For most family members, the biopsychosocial stress of dealing with substance abusers (who may or may not admit they have a problem) can often lead to stress-related health problems as well as reduced self-esteem and an erosion of the natural bonds that keep families together. Given that substance abuse is often linked to related issues such as domestic violence and emotional abuse, the risk of physical violence and related problems can be greater as well.

Much of the research into how substance abuse affects families has focused on child development, particularly how children handle dealing with parental substance abuse (whether the father, mother, or both). As you would expect, children exposed to childhood adversity such as parental substance abuse during their formative years typically have a high risk for developing serious emotional problems, including depression, social anxiety, and problem behaviors such as delinquency, self-harming, and suicide. Also, given their early exposure to drugs or alcohol as well as possible genetic influences, they are also at risk for becoming substance abusers themselves.

For that matter, even children who have been removed from the family home and placed in foster care due to parental substance abuse tend to be more at risk due to the disruptions in their normal family life and the stress that is often associated with these kinds of placements. As a result, the impact of parental substance abuse can continue to affect the emotional development of children even if they are no longer being directly exposed to it.

Unfortunately, most of the treatment services available for family members dealing with substance abuse tend to be concentrated in urban areas, which may make them hard to access for people in need who live further away. Groups such as Al-Anon can be found in many areas, which offer help for family members seeking information or support. For young people, there are programs such as Alateen and Teen Link, which offer help lines as well as an online chat service allowing direct contact with teen volunteers who are prepared to listen and find help.

Many inpatient and outpatient substance abuse treatment programs also provide services for family members needing emotional support and, in many cases, encourage family members to become part of the treatment process. Not only does this improve the odds of treatment success, but this also allows substance abusers and their families to repair their family connections.

28. Why is substance abuse so common in prisons?

In the United States alone, there are an estimated 2.2 million prisoners, making it the world leader in terms of the number of people incarcerated. Over the past four decades, largely as a result of "get tough" policies that appeal to voters, the number of people in jail has skyrocketed though many states are beginning to reconsider this trend. Not only are the overwhelming majority of these prisoners from economically disadvantaged backgrounds and often people of color, but approximately half of all prisoners also suffer from one or more mental health problems.

Many of these prisoners have serious mental health problems such as schizophrenia, which might once have been treated in psychiatric hospitals, but the lack of available treatment beds means that they are increasingly ending up in prison instead. In addition, drug and alcohol abuse is rampant inside prison walls, as much to cope with the grueling conditions as to self-medicate for other conditions for which they often do not receive treatment.

Over the past several decades, we have seen a sharp rise in people sent to prison for drug-related offenses. This often means that more and more prisoners are deeply involved in the drug subculture and often have the contacts they need for purchasing drugs on the outside that can then be smuggled in for profit.

Given the financial incentives for smuggling drugs into prisons, many prisoners and even some guards have been known to act as "mules" to bring drugs to paying inmates. Prisoners receiving psychiatric or pain medication can often be "muscled" or otherwise persuaded to sell or give their medication away for other inmates to use. It is also quite common for many prisoners to make "brews" in their cells by allowing fruit juices to ferment with sugar and other less-savory ingredients as "flavoring." While prison guards tend to be vigilant about potential infractions, prisoners are often ingenious in their methods of hiding their drug or alcohol stashes in their cells or other places in the prison. Considering the money that can be made selling drugs or other illegal items, it's hardly surprising that so many enterprising inmates devote time and effort to find new ways of evading prison security.

What this often means, especially in lower-security prisons, is a substance abuse problem that can be just as severe as what many of these same inmates may face outside of prison. It also places an added burden on those inmates who are trying to stay "clean" and avoid the drugs that have gotten them into trouble in the past.

Ironically, tobacco use is perfectly legal inside prisons and, since cigarettes can be freely purchased by inmates, they have become an informal currency that are often used to pay off gambling debts as well as being exchanged for other favors. Due to the stress of prison life, many inmates may find their need for tobacco, caffeine, or any other mind-altering substance sharply increased: a need that can often carry over into their life after prison as well.

29. What are the real costs of substance abuse to society?

As we've already seen in Question 6, there may be no real way of determining the real costs of substance abuse to society since the actual number of substance abusers may be impossible to determine. Still, even rough estimates suggest that the true costs of substance abuse can be astronomical. According to statistics compiled by the National Institute of Drug Abuse, the total cost of substance abuse is approximately $740 billion per year. Looking at those same statistics, about 40 percent of those total costs stem from tobacco alone, while an additional 33.6 percent is from alcohol. As for illegal drugs, they account only for 26.1 percent of the total (which still amounts to $193 billion a year). This does not include the costs resulting from prescription opioids, which can run to $79 billion per year.

When broken down further, the largest share of that $740 billion per year is from indirect costs. This is the cost due to lost work productivity, that is, time lost from work due to substance-related health problems or premature death. Since this can apply to family members of substance abusers as well, these indirect cost estimates likely underestimate the true economic impact of substance abuse. Also, these figures don't take into account the money people spend on alcohol, tobacco, or illegal drugs as well as many of the "intangible" costs resulting from mental suffering.

In looking at the direct costs of substance abuse on society, the biggest single expenditure deals with health care. This includes specialized treatment programs (whether inpatient or outpatient), emergency medical care, visits to the family doctor, and medication prescribed to treat substance abuse. These figures also factor in the cost of treating medical conditions that can be directly linked to substance use, including tobacco, so this includes treatment for different types of cancer that are nicotine related. Overall, this works out to $232 billion per year, with tobacco alone accounting for $168 billion.

And then there are the financial costs involved with law enforcement. Approximately 14 percent of the total cost associated with drugs and alcohol goes to maintaining police forces, the courts, and the prison system.

Though it's often hard to compare prison systems between different countries, there is certainly no question that the United States alone has more people in prison than any other nation. Of those, an estimated 85 percent are incarcerated due to drug- or alcohol-related offenses alone. Along with the cost of keeping all these prisoners behind bars, there is the cost involved in dealing with substance use inside prison as well (see previous question).

Even though there may be no conclusive way to measure the true costs of substance abuse to society, we can see that an astronomical amount is spent each year in one form or another. But the impact of substance abuse can't be weighed in financial costs alone: family members, including spouses, children, siblings, or parents, are certainly affected as well. The emotional toll this can take is in the form of increased stress, increased risk of domestic abuse, financial pressures, and the social stigma that often surrounds families of known drug or alcohol abusers. Whether directly or indirectly, the burden of dealing with addiction is something we all end up paying for eventually.

❖❖❖

Culture, Media, and Substance Abuse

30. How do different cultures view substance abuse?

As you are likely well aware, drug laws vary widely from country to country, and many substances that are highly illegal in some places can be freely used in others. Cannabis, for example, can be legally purchased and consumed in countries such as South Africa, Spain, and Uruguay. In the Netherlands, cannabis is routinely bought and smoked in "hashish shops" found in Amsterdam and other large cities, something that often confounds tourists from more-restrictive countries.

Cannabis possession has been decriminalized in many other countries and some U.S. states, though there are still restrictions on amounts of cannabis that can be legally purchased. For most other countries however, cannabis possession is restricted except for medical use, though many of these same countries have strong political movements pushing for decriminalization.

In recent years, many countries have also called for more liberal drug laws, allowing greater use of certain narcotics for medical purposes. They have also been calling for more safe injection sites where addicts can exchange needles under medical supervision to avoid infection or other health problems. This push toward greater drug liberalization is based on a move away from criminalizing drug abuse and treating it as a public health problem instead. For example, in 2001, Portugal became the first

European country to decriminalize possession of all drugs for personal use and, despite dire predictions, has seen a sharp drop in substance-related deaths and medical problems relating to substance use (more on that in Question 36).

Despite this greater liberalization, there are still many places with harsh penalties for drug or alcohol possession. In Saudi Arabia, for example, punishment for possession or use of alcohol can include public flogging, large fines, a prison sentence, or even death depending on the circumstances. According to Indonesian law, possession of marijuana can be punished by up to 20 years in prison, and people caught selling drugs are executed. While alcohol remains legal there, many legislators continue to push for a nationwide ban. Many other Muslim countries have similar drug laws, and countries such as Dubai have been known to deport travelers for having certain prescription medications that are perfectly legal elsewhere.

Other countries with a death penalty for drug traffickers include Vietnam, Malaysia, Iran, and Singapore. Whether or not someone in that country will be charged with drug trafficking often depends on *how much* of the illegal drug he or she possesses, something that has caught many tourists by surprise. Part of the reason why drug laws are so harsh in that part of the world is how close they are to Southeast Asia's Golden Triangle of opium-exporting countries and the ease with which drugs can be smuggled into neighboring countries.

And then there are drugs that are part of the religious or ethnic traditions of many cultures. In Peru, for example, tea made from coca leaves are widely used as a mild stimulant even though these leaves cannot be legally imported to the United States unless the cocaine content has been removed. Visitors to Peru can also take part in ayahuasca ceremonies, where native shamans lead them through vision quests while under the drug's influence. For that matter, peyote is a common part of vision quests in many Native American cultures, while cannabis has widespread ritual use in Rastafarian communities. Over the years, there has been frequent conflict between government drug laws and how they apply to religious practices involving controlled substances.

While laws and cultural traditions involving drug and alcohol use can vary widely from place to place, it is still important to recognize the medical and psychological problems that can result from addiction. This is why it is important to seek help from mental health professionals who are sensitive to cultural and religious differences and also to remain aware of the existing drug laws in any country you may live in or visit.

31. How effective is workplace and school drug testing in helping substance abusers?

In recent years, many workplaces and even schools have implemented random urine testing to catch drug users. These urine tests are designed to detect traces of drugs such as cannabis, cocaine, amphetamines, opioids, and phencyclidine (PCP). With random testing, even workers or students with no known drug history can be asked to provide a urine, hair, blood, or sweat sample.

While the legality of this kind of testing has been challenged in the courts, the U.S. Supreme Court ruled in 2002 that public schools have the authority to test students for drug use. This ruling specifically applies to all middle- and high school students and extends preexisting policies concerning drug testing for student athletes. The prime rationale for this kind of testing is to deter students from using drugs and to identify students who need treatment, though, with "zero tolerance" policies becoming more popular, students are often expelled or suspended as well.

Despite the Supreme Court ruling, not all schools will necessarily implement drug testing given that it is often expensive and difficult to introduce. According to one 2005 study, around 28 percent of all high schools carry out random drug testing, though athletes or other students engaged in competitive extracurricular activities are much more likely to undergo testing.

Drug testing in the workplace primarily focuses on workers who are engaged in jobs operating heavy machinery or who might otherwise endanger themselves or others by working under the influence of drugs. This includes transportation, safety, defense, and aviation companies. Industries regulated by the U.S. Department of Transportation are covered by federal and state legislation that requires regular testing. Other industries that can require drug or alcohol testing include hospitals, professional and amateur sports, schools, and universities, though, again, this can vary depending on local laws.

The popularity of workplace testing has led to the establishment of numerous commercial drug testing facilities offering a wide range of services, including urine and saliva testing, blood testing, hair and sweat testing, and even alcohol breath analysis. Though the quality often varies, most of these companies follow Substance Abuse and Mental Health Services Administration guidelines in testing for alcohol as well as such drugs as cannabis, most narcotics and opiates, and phencyclidine. Some companies may require more sensitive testing that can catch a much wider variety of drugs, including anabolic steroids, tranquilizers, and barbiturates.

For many of these drugs, there are specific detection windows during which drug testing can detect recent use. With alcohol, for example, urine or blood testing can only detect if alcohol has been consumed in the previous 24 hours, while hair testing can retain traces of alcohol up to 90 days after consumption. Hair testing can also be used to test for the presence of a wide range of narcotics for up to 90 days after use, though most testing focuses on blood, saliva, or urine.

Where and when companies can engage in drug and alcohol testing of employees often depends on what state and federal laws allow. In some states, drug screening is also permitted for job applicants as well as employees, even if they aren't in jobs that are potentially endangered by substance use. Testing can be required for employees offered a promotion, following an on-the-job accident, or simply if substance use is suspected. In the United States, substance abuse testing has also become mandatory for all federal parolees and people on probation.

Increased use of drug and alcohol testing has also led to more sophisticated ways of avoiding detection, often by substituting the sample to be tested with a "clean" sample that shows no evidence of substance use. There is also considerable controversy over the sensitivity of some of the more popular drug tests since certain prescription drugs, and even over-the-counter remedies, can lead to false positives that can result in employees being unfairly labeled as substance abusers. Even consuming poppy seeds (a common ingredient in many baked goods) prior to testing can lead to being identified as an opioid user.

Despite the controversy that continues to surround drug and alcohol testing in schools and workplaces, its use will almost certainly continue, at least in safety-sensitive industries where substance use can be life threatening as well as for athletes in competitions. While civil rights cases continue to challenge the right of schools or employers to use these tests, drug testing is rapidly becoming standard practice in more and more places.

32. Do zero tolerance policies work to control substance use?

A zero tolerance policy imposes strict penalties for any infraction deemed to violate rules of conduct. This also means that the people charged with enforcing the policy typically lack any kind of flexibility when it comes to imposing punishments. While these kinds of policies are often put in place to reflect a "get tough" philosophy, research tends to show that they do more harm than good in most settings.

In the United States, zero tolerance policies were introduced during the 1980s as part of the War on Drugs advocated by Presidents Ronald Reagan and George Bush. Aimed at drug users, zero tolerance policies, including the imposing of minimum sentences for drug possession, were intended as a way of reducing drug use by eliminating the demand rather than going after drug suppliers. It was during this same period that the number of people in prison rose dramatically as more and more drug users were given prison sentences instead of being allowed to enter treatment programs.

Zero tolerance policies have also become increasingly applied in schools and universities as a way of controlling substance use and other problem behaviors such as bullying or possession of a weapon. Unfortunately, given that school officials required to uphold the policy have no real flexibility in how it is applied, this can often mean that students can be expelled for even relatively minor infractions. Incidents in which even young children received severe punishments for bringing certain kinds of nonprescription medications to school are not uncommon, and school boards have faced lawsuits for upholding them.

The use of zero tolerance policies has also led to what the news media and social critics have called the "school to prison pipeline." This means that students from disadvantaged backgrounds are often deprived of an education or any kind of treatment for substance abuse and, as a result, are more likely to end up in prison. The increased presence of police officers in school also leads to an increased risk of arrest for behavior that might have been treated more leniently and effectively by the school administration. Research continues to show significant racial differences in terms of which students are most likely to be targeted by zero tolerance, including African American, Hispanic/Latino, and Native American boys.

But the problems linked to zero tolerance aren't limited to schools alone. These have had similar outcomes in work settings, especially when the zero tolerance policies are put in place as part of a get tough strategy rather than any actual proof that these policies are effective. Though it seems unlikely that zero tolerance policies will be phased out in the foreseeable future given their popularity, the question of how useful they really are will continue to be a source of controversy in the years to come.

33. Can media stories about substance abuse do more harm than good?

Considering the large number of recent news stories describing positive drug experiences, some advocates are suggesting that psychedelic drugs are becoming more popular. Not only are drugs such as LSD, psilocybin, and MDMA being used as therapy tools to assist people with mental health issues, but news stories about "cognitive enhancers" that can reportedly improve memory and attention have sparked an increased demand for these drugs even though potential risks are not well understood. Stories about "mind expanding" drugs such as ayahuasca and peyote may also lead to people concluding that such drugs are harmless and, as a result, may lead to these drugs (which are still illegal in many places) to be misused.

On the other hand, we have also seen numerous "moral panics" that have arisen due to stories about new designer drugs and the danger they supposedly represent to drug users. In 2010, news stories in the United Kingdom raised alarm about numerous drug deaths said to be caused by mephedrone, a synthetic stimulant that was legal at the time. Antidrug advocates called for an immediate ban on the drug as it was said to be responsible for the deaths of dozens of adolescents.

Around the same time, a well-publicized press conference by a UK police force blamed several recent deaths on "m-cat" as they called mephedrone. They also urged anyone who had recently taken it to go to hospital "as a matter of urgency." Wikipedia articles about mephedrone and related drugs were updated to reflect the new fears, as well as much of the misconceptions that were spreading. Since many journalists relied on Wikipedia and related sources for information on mephedrone, this added to the drug panic across the United Kingdom. Largely as a result of political pressure, mephedrone became illegal in most European countries that same year.

In spite of the media outcry, some social media critics now suggest that the moral panic over mephedrone was largely overblown and that the deaths that were supposedly due to mephedrone overdose actually occurred for other reasons. In many instances, virtually any death involving young people tended to be blamed on mephedrone even though toxicological screenings later showed that they had no trace of it in their systems. Though some scientists argued against a ban at the time, they were largely overruled and, in some cases, fired.

In much the same way that mephedrone became labeled as a dangerous drug, media stories about other designer drugs have resulted in new moral panics and calls for tougher drug laws as a result. How reliable these news stories are needs to be carefully weighed by anyone trying to learn more about these drugs and whether or not these moral panics are actually justified. Unfortunately, panic and hype help sell newspapers, something that we all need to remember.

34. Is there an online substance abuse subculture?

In much the same way online gambling and pornographic sites provide easy access to content and services that are often illegal in many places, the past 10 years has seen an explosion of new sites that allow people to purchase drugs as well. These sites can include online pharmacies selling opioids and other kinds of medication online. With these online pharmacies, opioids, barbiturates, stimulants, and even "date rape" drugs are often offered at low prices though the customers often face problems due to the quality of the drugs being offered, not to mention the legality of these kinds of purchases.

Other drug sites provide recipes, hidden links, and helpful hints by drug users worldwide, as well as forums or bulletin boards offering advice on how to avoid getting caught by authorities. While drug enforcement agencies try to shut these sites down on a routine basis, the operators often find ways to bypass laws either by posting from countries where the sites are legal or by relying on darknets to avoid arrest.

Darknets are specialized networks that can be accessed only with certain kinds of security browsers and related software. Along with allowing users to hide from political repression, darknet markets can also be used to purchase a wide range of illegal products though how secure these networks really are remains controversial. Many of these darknets are part of the "Deep Web" and can provide a black market for drug trafficking, though drug enforcement agencies worldwide have been vigilant in shutting them down.

For people who might be tempted to visit these different sites, there are some important warnings that should be considered. Not only are many of the drugs being offered online highly illegal, but the vendors themselves may be confidence artists trying to solicit credit card or other payment information for identity theft. Anyone trying to order these products, even the ones that are described as "legal highs" or "safe pharmaceuticals," run the risk of becoming part of a police investigation into the vendor, not to mention facing charges themselves.

Even if the vendor does deliver as promised, there are no guarantees that the product will be safe for human consumption. Much like drug pushers in local communities, the delivered product could be contaminated with potentially harmful ingredients, or even being completely bogus (such as not containing any of the active ingredients that would make them effective).

In one recent example, investigators looking at online pharmacies selling Xenical, an FDA-approved weight loss drug, found that the product received from three different online pharmacies didn't contain the active ingredient that was supposed to be present. Instead, the capsules advertised as Xenical contained another ingredient completely which happens to be a controlled substance (and potentially harmful).

Even visiting online drug user bulletin boards or forums offering drug advice or recipes could be dangerous since many of these recipes or "advice" can often be dangerous, whether due to misinformation or being deliberately posted as a malicious prank. This is why all online stories about some new "high" that is guaranteed to be both legal and safe to use need to be viewed with skepticism. While responsible drug sites do exist, many others are there to sell drugs, drug equipment, books containing information about drugs, or some other product that users tend to be better off without. The Directory of Resources contains some useful sites to learn more about substance abuse and treatment though it is important to do your own research before accepting any online claims at face value.

35. Do drug prevention programs work?

When the "Just Say No" campaign was launched in the 1980s as part of the U.S. war on drugs, it was intended as an effective way of teaching children and adolescents to resist peer pressure and stay off of drugs. With public support from well-known figures such as then-First Lady Nancy Reagan, slogans such as "Just Say No" became part of popular American pop culture and even found their way overseas as antidrug programs took root in countries such as the United Kingdom and Australia.

Still, many critics argued that relying on slogans and catchphrases was far too simplistic to address the real challenges involved in combating substance abuse and, for the most part, they were probably right. While the 1990s saw a significant drop in recreational drug use among adolescents and young adults, they also saw record numbers of overdoses and the rise of a new opioid epidemic. Actual research examining the impact the Just Say No campaign had on drug use in the United States and other countries tended to be ambivalent at best.

In explaining why Just Say No appeared to be so ineffective, critics suggested that the message was too simplistic and also placed the burden of dealing with a massive underground industry solely on individual drug users rather than relying on improved social policies and better access to treatment. Programs based on Just Say No also encouraged total drug abstinence and focused on illegal drugs while largely ignoring legally sanctioned drugs.

While broad-based programs such as Just Say No don't seem to work that well, school- and community-based substance education programs are increasingly taking their place. Rather than relying on simplistic messages and warnings about drug laws, many of these programs have started focusing more on making children and adolescents more aware of how to avoid being harmed by drugs and alcohol, an approach known as "drug literacy." Many of these programs also focus on more achievable goals rather than assuming that drug or alcohol use can be completely eliminated.

Another goal of drug literacy programs is to make potential users more aware of the mixed messages they often receive when it comes to drug or alcohol use. For example, children often encounter ads on television, radio, and the press encouraging people to drink alcohol as a way of enjoying "the good life." Also, while drugs such as heroin are often denounced as dangerous and illegal, pain medications that contain many of the same ingredients continue to be advertised in many places. There is also the confusion that can arise due to differences in drug laws from one jurisdiction to another, not to mention the issues surrounding medical marijuana, methadone treatment, and the increasing push to legalize cannabis around the world.

To help students gain a better understanding of drug literacy, schools that offer these programs use open discussions on different drug topics and can also assign projects involving issues that students find important. This teaches students to think critically about their own drug-related beliefs and attitudes and to make their own decisions about how to function in social situations where they are likely to encounter drugs and alcohol.

Though drug literacy programs remain controversial, especially with many parents who equate these programs with "encouraging" drug and alcohol use, they are often more effective than total abstinence approaches such as Just Say No. Greater acceptance of drug literacy programs may be an important step in eliminating many of the health and social problems linked to substance use that we now face.

36. Should drug use be legalized?

Though there have been long periods in history when drugs such as cannabis, opium, cocaine, and heroin could be legally purchased, the social problems that often developed as a result have led to many of the modern drug laws that remain in place in most countries. As we have already seen in Question 30, these drug laws vary widely from place to place and drugs that are banned in some countries can be legally purchased in others. It is also debatable whether tough drug laws are actually effective in curbing substance abuse and many of the social problems that go with it.

In 2001, Portugal became the first European country to decriminalize possession of all drugs for personal use, though, contrary to popular belief, people can still face penalties ranging from confiscation of their drugs, fines, or community service. Portugal's revised drug laws have also led to a sharp rise in treatment facilities as well as increased use of methadone maintenance programs and harm reduction policies intended to reduce many of the known health risks associated with substance use. Largely as a result of the new liberalized drug policy, Portugal has seen a sharp rise in the number of people receiving drug treatment and a significant decrease in new HIV cases stemming from IV drug use.

At the same time however, Portugal has also seen a significant rise in cannabis, heroin, and cocaine use, though similar increases were also reported in neighboring countries that haven't changed their drug laws. There has also been a sharp drop in use of "legal highs" such as synthetic marijuana and other designer drugs.

Perhaps most important, Portugal has the lowest rate of drug-related overdose deaths in all of Europe. According to recent statistics, the rate of lethal overdoses in Portugal is only three per million. By comparison, drug deaths in the United Kingdom is 44.6 per million while rates, in the rest of Europe range from 10.2 per million in the Netherlands to 126.8 per million in Estonia. The overall average in the European Union is 17.2 per million.

Despite this sharp drop in overdose deaths, health authorities in Portugal warn that this drop has leveled off in recent years as more autopsies involving suspected drug deaths are being carried out in that country. Also, as Dr. Joao Goulao, the architect of Portugal's drug decriminalization policy, pointed out in a 2015 interview with the *Washington Post*, "It's very difficult to identify a causal link between decriminalization by itself and the positive tendencies we have seen."

Still, despite the dire predictions of many conservatives, the overall outcome of the drug decriminalization experiment in Portugal has been quite positive, something advocates for more liberal drug laws in other countries have also noted. Though it seems unlikely that many countries will be following Portugal's example, at least in the near-future, countries such as Canada have announced plans to legalize cannabis for recreational use as well as advocating a push for greater decriminalization of other drugs. Whether or not Portugal's success with drug decriminalization will be reproduced in other places still remains to be seen.

37. Should recreational use of marijuana be legal?

Though cannabis was widely available until the first two decades of the 20th century, it was also one of the first drugs to be banned in most countries around the world. Despite prominent exceptions, possession of even small amounts of marijuana or hashish often meant harsh penalties depending on where the arrest occurred (including death penalty in some Islamic countries). These harsh sentences were often justified with the familiar argument that marijuana was a "gateway drug" which needed to be banned to keep it from corrupting "impressionable" young people.

But this is changing rapidly in many places. Not only have medical marijuana programs and clinics been established in numerous countries (and 29 U.S. states to date), but some jurisdictions have gone even further. In 2013, Uruguay became the first country to legalize the sale, cultivation, and distribution of marijuana, and many other countries, including Canada, are expected to follow suit in the near-future. Recreational marijuana use has also been made legal in Alaska, California, Colorado, Oregon, Washington, and the District of Columbia, with advocates in other states calling for the same.

Despite these changes, the issues surrounding marijuana legalization continue to be hotly debated, both at the federal level and in most states with stringent drug laws. Not surprisingly, politicians and activists opposing legalization are using recent statistics showing that marijuana use is on the rise among adolescents to push for a universal ban. But surveys also show that this rising trend is due to changing attitudes and greater acceptance of marijuana use among adults.

In states such as Oregon and Colorado, advertisements for marijuana products have become increasingly common, and outlets where they can be purchased can be found in most places. In addition, anyone 21 years or older can grow plants for their own use, though the amount they can take with them while traveling is still limited. Visitors and tourists can also use marijuana legally though they are still subject to arrest if they are caught with any in their possession once they travel to another state.

Though it's probably too soon to evaluate whether legalization of marijuana will have a significant impact on overall drug use for adults and adolescents, early studies have shown no real evidence of problems developing so far. In spite of this initial success however, the barriers against wide-scale legalization remain at the international level, and the penalties for cannabis use can still be severe in many places. For that matter, illegal trafficking of cannabis continues worldwide, with marijuana and hashish accounting for up to 75 percent of the total number of seizures for all drugs in Europe and North America alone.

Even as legalization campaigns continue, the political controversy and the bureaucratic barriers currently in place mean that little real change is likely to occur at the international level, at least for the next few decades. That means that marijuana and hashish will go on being illegal in most places and users will need to be aware of that.

＊

Treatment, Prevention, and Life after Substance Abuse

38. What are some of the most common forms of treatment for children and adults who abuse drugs and alcohol?

There are a wide range of different treatment options available for help-ing child, adolescent, and adult substance abusers. Still, there is no one-size-fits-all approach, and the treatment substance users may receive will often depend on what kind of drugs they are abusing, the symptoms they happen to be showing, their life history, and the treatment progress they are making over time.

For most substance users, whether they are adolescents or adults, treat-ment usually begins with an evaluation to determine how to proceed and also to start developing a treatment plan (see Question 41). This is basi-cally a road map that will help guide people through the treatment pro-cess. Also, depending on how severe the substance problem actually is and the kind of withdrawal effects users may be experiencing, a period of drug or alcohol detox is often required as well to help stabilize substance users and wean them off whatever they have been taking. As you will see in Question 40, detox can often require inpatient monitoring as well as round-the-clock medical care in many cases.

Whether or not detox is required, the next step in treatment involves one-to-one sessions with an addictions counselor. The main purpose of individual treatment is to make clients comfortable enough to be willing to open up about substance use and other related issues. It is also through individual sessions that clients can start talking about other issues that may be contributing to their substance use. This can include having a history of childhood physical or sexual abuse, posttraumatic symptoms, family concerns, social anxiety, and so on. Many clients may prefer to deal exclusively with individual counseling, while others may prefer to move into group treatment as soon as possible.

One of the advantages of individual counseling is the added privacy that it provides. This means that clients can open up in a way they might not feel comfortable doing in a group setting. Individual counseling can be either open ended or with a fixed number of sessions. Open-ended treatment means that sessions will continue until such time that the client is seen as ready to try group treatment. In addition to individual counseling, people in therapy may be seen in family counseling sessions with participating family members to learn how to work together to overcome substance abuse.

For many substance users who have successfully completed individual counseling and who feel ready to talk about their substance use more openly, the next step is to join a therapy group. The type of therapy offered often depends on what the person in treatment hopes to achieve. Groups can include the following:

- *Psychoeducation training programs*—Much as the name suggests, these programs focus on educating substance users about their substance use and the barriers they may face in overcoming addiction. Training modules can include anger management, relaxation training, good nutrition and exercise, and meditation.
- *Skill development programs*—Using an interactive training approach allowing group members to share their own insights and ideas, these group sessions focus on training members to handle anger effectively, learning about relapse prevention techniques, becoming better parents, manage finances properly, and recognizing the triggers that can lead to substance use.
- *Cognitive behavioral psychotherapy* (CBT)—In a CBT group, members are trained in how to recognize and change maladaptive beliefs and behaviors that can reinforce substance use. One of the central principles of CBT is to learn how to anticipate problems and develop self-control using effective coping strategies. Cognitive behavioral strategies can include cognitive restructuring, problem-solving, stress inoculation training, relaxation training, mindfulness, and relapse prevention techniques.

While most substance users can receive treatment on a weekly basis, people with long-standing substance abuse problems and a history of relapses may require much more intensive treatment than what is usually offered. It can also mean being treated in an inpatient facility to reduce the temptation that might come from living out in the community where drugs or alcohol can be easily obtained. Substance abusers can also attend treatment in conjunction with drug or alcohol detoxification to control withdrawal symptoms.

Even after treatment is completed, therapists and their patients need to decide on what will happen next. Many users who have completed treatment and manage to remain drug or alcohol free may choose to attend maintenance treatment sessions with their counselor on a monthly or bimonthly basis. This allows the counselor to monitor the progress being made as well as giving patients the chance to review material covered during the treatment sessions and share details of new concerns as they arise. It is also important for users who have completed treatment to remember that the risk of falling off the wagon will always be present and to avoid the kind of situations or pressures that could lead to a relapse. Many of the different treatment options available to drug and alcohol users will be covered in more detail in the next few sections.

39. Can't drug or alcohol users just quit cold turkey?

For many drug or alcohol users who may not accept how severe their problem really is, the idea that they can just quit on their own without any kind of medical help seems simple enough. Unfortunately, it can also be extremely dangerous.

Though it's hard to say how the term "cold turkey" first came to be applied to addicts, the actual success of this kind of approach to overcoming substance abuse tends to be mixed at best. While quitting cold turkey is possible, the risks involved, especially for people who have been abusing alcohol, benzodiazepines, or other drugs for a long time, can be potentially fatal in some cases.

How dangerous this can be often depends on a range of factors, including the type of drug used, how long the addiction has been going on, and whether or not there are additional medical or mental health problems that can add to the trauma involved.

With some drugs for example, people undergoing detox may need to be restrained due to potentially violent behavior resulting from emotional agitation, psychosis, or acute suicidal thoughts. For people with chronic pain problems who have become addicted to opioids, quitting cold turkey can be doubly dangerous since they are forced to deal with severe pain in addition to the withdrawal symptoms. Abrupt opioid withdrawal can also make users much more sensitive to pain in general.

While alcohol is often the drug that people are most likely to try stopping cold turkey, the consequences can be even more dangerous than for other addictive substances. For example, long-time alcohol abusers who stop cold turkey can develop a serious condition known as delirium tremens (DTs). Symptoms for DTs include rapid mental confusion, shaking, sweating, and, at times, visual hallucinations. Seizures and an abnormally high body temperature can also set in, which may be fatal if left untreated. Since the "half-life" for alcohol is relatively long, it usually takes several days after the last drink for DTs to set in.

Once the symptoms begin, they can last for three days or more and often require intensive hospital care to monitor for medical complications. While DTs is usually found only in 10 percent of alcohol withdrawal cases, anyone quitting alcohol cold turkey should still consider medical supervision. Similar problems have also been observed in people quitting benzodiazepines and barbiturates, making quitting cold turkey a very bad idea for these particular drugs.

Though the symptoms seen in people abruptly quitting other drugs such as cocaine, amphetamines, and nicotine are usually not as severe, they can still be traumatic enough to make many users conclude that their substance use is untreatable and, as a result, they often end up relapsing. In addition, quitting cold turkey can cause users to lose the physical tolerance they once had for the drugs they used, all of which means that starting up their drug use again at the levels they were taking before quitting can often be lethal since their bodies can no longer tolerate the same dosage as before.

As you can see, quitting cold turkey is not something to be entered into lightly. At the very least, anyone considering this way of getting off drugs or alcohol should get medical advice first to determine the best approach. For people dealing with long-term substance use, there are safe options, including drug or alcohol detoxification. More on this is discussed in the following question.

40. What is drug or alcohol detoxification?

For people dealing with severe drug or alcohol abuse and a longtime pattern of substance use, the first stage of treatment often involves drug or alcohol detoxification (detox for short). This basically involves helping the body overcome cravings and withdrawal effects under medical supervision, usually on an inpatient basis. While outpatient detox can help with less-severe types of addictions, the people who need detox most commonly need full-time medical supervision while they learn to handle what is happening to them.

The detox process usually begins with a careful evaluation of the kind of addiction a person is experiencing as well as identifying any underlying mental or physical health problems that could make detox more difficult. During this evaluation stage, people considering detox are asked questions about how long they have been addicted, which drugs they have been taking (especially if they are polysubstance abusers with multiple addictions), whether they have other mental or physical health problems, or how long it has been since their last dose. The answers they provide to these questions determine when the detox can begin and how long it would be likely to last. With some drugs, for example, the half-life can be very short and withdrawal effects can begin within a few hours, though with other drugs, this can take much longer. Users also need to be prepared for the kind of symptoms they are likely to experience so that proper medical intervention can be used if needed.

Considering that the withdrawal symptoms that can be experienced might include agitation, hallucinations, seizures, and suicidal thoughts or actions, patients in detox often require careful monitoring with security to keep them from harming themselves or others. Though the goal of detox is to help addicts overcome their addiction, medical doctors often prescribe medications that make the withdrawal process easier. For people dealing with opioid withdrawal, for example, detox can often include treatment with methadone or buprenorphine to control the cravings. With benzodiazepine detox, patients typically keep taking the drug they have been using but in gradually smaller amounts as well as switching to a less-addictive substitute.

On the other hand, people undergoing detox from cocaine or methamphetamines may be given carefully regulated doses of benzodiazepines to control withdrawal. While this is still potentially addictive, there are no real medical alternatives at present to help make the withdrawal process less traumatic. Fortunately, withdrawal from benzodiazepines is relatively easy once detox is completed.

Along with the problems associated with physiological withdrawal, there are psychological withdrawal effects to be considered. People who have become dependent on drugs or alcohol to help deal with stress, depression, or anxiety may become more agitated as they realize that they can no longer rely on their usual coping method. This is why many substance rehabilitation programs combine detox with supportive counseling, group or individual psychotherapy, or stress management training.

Given the medical and psychological problems that can arise, anyone considering detox should get medical advice first. Even for people who don't believe their addiction is that severe, the withdrawal symptoms that can occur are often hard to predict. For this reason alone, detox should be considered only if 24-hour care and/or regular medical monitoring is available.

Unfortunately, detox is not an option for everyone considering the amount of time and cost that is often involved. Many people cannot afford to spend weeks or months as an inpatient and, given that these programs are usually found in private clinics or hospitals that may not be covered by some health plans, may not have the resources to afford this kind of expense. Though short-term detox programs are also available, they may not be advisable for people with severe substance abuse problems. Consult with your addictions counselor about the best option.

41. What is a treatment plan?

There is no such thing as a one-size-fits-all treatment for substance abuse. The kind of treatment needed will vary widely depending on the age of the abuser, whether there are related mental health problems that also need to be treated, how far back the substance abuse history goes, whether the abuser is suffering from medical problems that can complicate recovery, and whether the treatment professional needs to deal with other issues such as childhood abuse or trauma.

For anyone seeking treatment, the first step begins with meeting with an addictions counselor and formulating a *treatment plan* that outlines the goals that need to be met and the type of treatment that might be needed to achieve those goals. Once the goals are laid out, the therapist and the client then establish priorities, that is, which goals need to be met first and which can be addressed later. While the primary goal of treatment will be to overcome addiction, there are also going to be secondary goals that can include improving family relationships, learning to be more social, and repairing problems at work or school that may have originated because of substance use. As part of the treatment plan, the therapist and the client also need to work out which goals can be achieved in the short term (i.e., within the next six months) and which in the long term. Achieving the short-term goals can often provide treatment clients with the confidence they need to stay in treatment.

The important point to remember is that no two treatment plans are the same. Even if two people with similar problems enter treatment at the same time, the goals they will set are often very different. Because they have different life experiences, the problems they will be trying to overcome, as well as their individual strengths and weaknesses, are going to shape the kind of treatment they need.

With many treatment plans, the first step involves developing a *problem list*. As you might expect, this means itemizing those problems that the patient happens to be experiencing *at that point in time*. Over the course of treatment, the problem list is going to change as old problems become manageable and new problems crop up. In developing the problem list, the patient needs to be able to describe the problem clearly and also to come up with concrete ways of measuring the progress they will make in dealing with that problem.

For example, the problem could be stated as "I can't stay sober for long when I'm at parties." The concrete evidence for this problem could include complaints from friends or family members about the kind of behavior that comes out after having too many drinks. Additional evidence for this problem could include difficulties with the law that develop due to driving home drunk or getting into fights after too much of this social drinking. Other problems that can go on the problem list include emotional issues such as social anxiety or depression.

The next step is to outline the *short-term and long-term goals* that patients need to meet to get their abuse under control. While overcoming chronic problems such as drug or alcohol abuse can be considered long-term goals, patients and their therapists also need to identify short-term goals. Along with acting as signposts that indicate the progress being made, achieving these goals help patients gain the confidence they need to continue in treatment and learn how to get their lives back on track.

As one example, a treatment plan for someone attending court-ordered counseling following a conviction for impaired driving might develop short-term goals such as "identifying the circumstances that led up to the impaired driving and learning to recognize them in future." If the drinking is part of a pattern of chronic drinking in social situations, a short-term goal would be to attend a party or social gathering without taking a single drink. Another short-term goal would be to become sensitive to the social cues that can make the patient more likely to drink and/or identifying friends who are more likely to support their plan to stay sober.

Once the goals are established, the next step is to outline the type of treatment to be used to help patients achieve the goals. Over the course of the treatment period, the treatment plan is periodically reviewed to determine how successful the patient has been at meeting the original goals.

As these goals are met, the treatment plan often changes as well depending on what is happening in the patient's life and the progress that ends up being made. Since relapses are often going to happen, patients are encouraged to treat these episodes as learning opportunities and form new goals that can help them regain their confidence and learn to avoid relapses in future.

Even after the treatment ends and the patient manages to meet all the planned goals, the treatment plan can continue to act as a road map for future progress by outlining the different ways that patients can maintain the progress they have made. This can include maintenance sessions once every six months so patients can review what they have learned and establishing additional long-term goals that patients can continue to try achieving over time. Also, many opioid addicts may need regular methadone maintenance treatment or some other form of drug treatment to manage withdrawal symptoms over the long run.

42. What is relapse prevention?

First introduced in the 1980s, relapse prevention (RP) has become one of the most important substance abuse treatment approaches used today. Based on the model developed by psychologists G. Alan Marlatt and Judith R. Gordon, RP focuses on the different emotional and situational influences that can increase the risk of a substance abuser returning to drug or alcohol use despite a desire to stay sober. Since drug and alcohol rehabilitation statistics tend to show that users have a 50–90 percent chance of relapsing over time, it is more important than ever to identify effective strategies to prevent relapsing or, if the relapse has already occurred, to help users return to sobriety.

While we tend to think of a relapse as someone "falling off the wagon" abruptly, the RP model actually describes relapsing as a gradual process that can occur over weeks or even months before a user actually begins using drugs or alcohol again. According to research, this process tends to follow three basic stages: (1) emotional relapse, (2) mental relapse, and (3) physical relapse.

In emotional relapse, users who once depended on drugs or alcohol to manage stress may find themselves dealing with a stressful situation that their substance-free lifestyle hasn't yet equipped them to handle. For someone who once relied on alcohol or drugs to deal with anxiety or depression, being faced with new pressures and not having proper coping mechanisms in place to handle these pressures can lead to greater emotional distress. Such distress can often catch substance users off guard since they may not realize they are letting things get out of control until too late. People going through emotional relapse often find themselves feeling more "on edge," feeling more depressed or angry, or lying awake at night because they are unable to sleep.

Allowing these feelings to go unchecked for too long often leads to the next stage, *mental relapse*. This is when thoughts about using drugs or alcohol again become more frequent and increasingly harder to deal with. Given the biological roots of substance abuse, spending too much time in the mental relapse stage can lead to the addiction centers of the brain becoming more active. As a result, they become more aware of renewed cravings and increased awareness of the old triggers that can lead to substance use. People experiencing mental relapse can also begin sabotaging their efforts to stay sober, whether by skipping treatment sessions or putting themselves in risky situations where substance use becomes more likely. They may also start making what is known as *apparently irrelevant decisions* that can put them at greater risk (such as taking a new route home from work or school that *happens* to pass by a bar or place where they used to buy drugs).

After emotional and mental relapse comes the final stage: physical relapse and a return to drug or alcohol use. For people who experience a relapse, this can often be seen as a sign that the addiction is too strong, and any effort to stay clean is doomed to failure. With RP, any relapse is treated as a learning experience, which can be used to recognize how to avoid it from happening again in future. This is known as prolapse, or the process of turning away from destructive behavior patterns and making positive life changes. By learning about the different stages of relapse, people receiving RP training learn different coping strategies they can use to disrupt emotional and mental relapse stages and prevent physical relapse from occurring.

Another goal of RP training is learning to recognize the different kinds of high-risk situations that can encourage relapsing. For example, *intrapersonal high-risk situations* can occur when users are dealing with negative emotions such as anger, anxiety, loneliness, frustration, or even boredom. These situations are often brought on by emotional reactions to external events, such as being angry about an impending layoff, feeling pressure due to problems at school, and not having anything worthwhile to do.

Then there are *interpersonal high-risk situations* that involve conflicts with other people, whether family, friends, or strangers. The negative emotions that can occur following a fight with a family member, a poor job evaluation, or daily hassles that seem about to spill out of control can dramatically increase the risk of relapse. For that matter, even situations that can result in positive emotions can lead to temptation. This can include social gatherings where the temptation to drink or use drugs can be increased.

With all of these high-risk situations, the risk of relapse often depends on the kind of coping strategies that can be used to defuse the emotional and behavioral triggers that can occur, Numerous research studies have shown the effectiveness of RP training in dealing with different forms of addiction though it appears to work best for drug and alcohol addiction. Still, like all new skills, it takes time and effort to learn how to use RP coping strategies and make them part of daily life. For this reason, RP isn't intended to be a stand-alone treatment approach, and many substance users can also benefit from combining RP with other treatment programs.

43. Do twelve-step programs really work?

When Bill Wilson and Robert Holbrook Smith founded the original twelve-step program, Alcoholics Anonymous (AA) in 1935, they intended it as a way of helping people overcome addiction as part of a larger group of like-minded individuals. With that in mind, they incorporated the twelve steps and the twelve traditions that go with them into a book published in 1939 that has since become a bible for the entire movement.

According to the twelve steps, people joining AA or one of the other twelve-step programs need to acknowledge that their alcohol or drug use is out of control and that they need help to overcome it. Based on the original twelve-step model, members work to overcome addiction by developing themselves physically, mentally, and spiritually. This includes the need to make amends to anyone who has been hurt in the past by a member's substance abuse and to accept a new code of behavior that involves taking responsibility for any harm that occurs. While the twelve steps and traditions originally had a strong religious component, that is, members turning their will and lives over to God, this has changed over the years to focus on personal growth.

Through regular meetings with volunteer leaders and fellow addicts, members are able to discuss personal issues candidly and anonymously.

Each new member also receives individual guidance through a sponsor, a more experienced member who can guide recruits through the twelve steps as well as to help with crises as they occur. Any established member can be a sponsor so long as he or she has a sponsor as well and has already gone through all twelve steps in the program. While AA and its fellow organizations are typically run by volunteers, members in need of professional treatment can be referred to programs in the local community as well.

With millions of members and well over 100,000 groups worldwide, AA remains the most successful of the twelve-step programs and has acted as a model for numerous other groups. These include groups such as Narcotics Anonymous (NA), Cocaine Anonymous (CA), and Crystal Meth Anonymous and has also been adapted for the treatment of compulsive behaviors, including Gamblers Anonymous, Overeaters Anonymous, and Sex Addicts Anonymous. There are also auxiliary groups formed to help family members of addicts, including Al-Anon, Alateen, and Adult Children of Alcoholics.

Still, despite the popularity of twelve-step programs, research studies looking at how effective they are in curbing substance abuse have reported mixed results over the years. Given that AA is the best known of the twelve-step programs and has the most members, most of the studies conducted to date have focused on its value in curbing alcohol abuse. Most studies comparing AA to control groups suggest that it is at least as effective as other treatment programs. Still, how much people benefit from AA often depends on how involved they are, that is, how often they go to meetings, how well they interact with other volunteers, and so on.

In recent years, there has also been considerable controversy over whether AA is as effective as supporters claim. Addiction specialist Dr. Lance Dodes published a book in 2014 suggesting that only 5–8 percent of AA members remain sober for longer than a year. In response, critics have argued that Dodes used flawed calculations to obtain the 5–8 percent figure and that research studies have been much more supportive of the AA model.

According to newer member surveys released by AA World Services, only about 40 percent of AA members attending programs for less than a year will remain sober and active in the program for another year. On the other hand, 90 percent of members staying in the program for five years or more will continue to stay active and sober for at least one more year.

Though twelve-step programs may not be suitable for everyone needing treatment for substance abuse, the popularity of AA, NA, CA, and similar groups can't be denied. People considering joining a local twelve-step group should discuss other treatment options with an addictions coun-selor as well as attend a few meetings to see if the twelve-step model is something they might want to follow.

44. What is harm reduction?

Harm reduction is the overall name for a series of public health policies intended to reduce many of the negative consequences associated with drug use. It's also used as the name for the social justice movement that promotes better protections for drug users. Recognizing that making drug use illegal is simply leading to more people suffering from overdoses and drug-related health problems, harm reduction focuses on teaching users responsible drug use that can minimize risk.

Among the harm reduction projects that have shown significant suc-cess are (1) *supervised injection sites,* where users can inject drugs under hygienic conditions; (2) needle and syringe exchange programs, where users can obtain sterile needles and hypodermics; (3) drug education programs providing basic information about safe drug use, and referrals to treatment; and (4) opioid substitution therapy, of which methadone maintenance therapy is the most well known. There are also "managed alcohol programs" in which homeless chronic alcoholics can be served small amounts of alcohol to keep them from drinking unsafe alternatives such as mouthwash, industrial alcohol, or household chemicals in order to get a "buzz."

The appeal of these harm reduction programs is that they offer a hassle-free and healthy environment where addicts consume drugs or alcohol without running many of the health risks often found in street people. Safe injection sites can be effective since they offer medical care, including treatment with naloxone, to prevent overdosing. Research has also shown that these sites can help reduce the street crime linked to drug and alcohol. Since the late 1990s, safe injection sites and other harm reduction programs have sprung into operation across numerous coun-tries, including the Netherlands, Australia, Canada, Germany, Spain, Norway, and Luxembourg, and are spreading to other countries as well.

While many U.S. cities have called for harm reduction programs to be established in recent years, the issue continues to be controversial con-sidering the widespread support for tougher drug laws that would ensure these programs stay illegal. Despite the strong opposition to these sites, there have been numerous task forces looking into the issue that suggest safe injection sites as a way of curbing overdose deaths. In addition, studies have largely disproven many of the objections raised about safe injection sites and similar programs, particularly the claim that these programs can increase illegal behavior linked to drug and alcohol use.

Given the proven effectiveness of harm reduction policies in preventing overdoses and other health problems stemming from substance abuse, many countries that already have these sites are quickly expanding their programs to cover even more cities and high-risk areas. Despite active opposition from antidrug agencies and social critics, the social benefits of harm reduction seem clear. Whether that will be enough to overcome political resistance remains to be seen.

45. What is cognitive behavioral therapy?

"Cognitive behavioral therapy" (CBT) is an overall term describing a range of problem-oriented psychotherapy techniques focusing on identifying and changing harmful thoughts and behaviors. Unlike more traditional forms of psychotherapy, CBT clients and their therapists work together in an active partnership to explore the negative thoughts, feelings, and behaviors that can underlie substance use.

How these negative beliefs develop is usually determined by the kind of drug being used, whether there are other health problems such as chronic pain or depression, and the social and cultural experiences that can shape addictive behavior. Though CBT tends to focus on current thought patterns and behaviors, people dealing with other mental health issues or early abuse may also explore how these issues may be sabotaging their recovery.

Part of the appeal of CBT is its flexibility. Not only can it be administered either individually or in treatment groups, but CBT can also be adapted for use in couples or family therapy or in dealing with clients with special needs. Along with CBT programs for children and adolescents, there are treatment programs aimed at adults dealing childhood sexual or physical abuse, domestic violence, or other issues that might lead to addiction.

Typically, individual or group CBT sessions can range from 45 minutes to over an hour per week. Despite having a strong educational component, clients and therapists can also use CBT sessions to exchange information and ideas about how the treatment is going. In a real sense, they are working together as part of the therapy process to find real solutions to drug and alcohol abuse.

In addition to the treatment sessions, clients receive homework assignments with exercises to apply what they learn in treatment. The lessons covered in these assignments can include learning to identify negative thoughts and behaviors that might increase the risk of substance use, learning coping strategies to deal with potential sources of stress, and learning effective ways of coping with cravings or self-defeating thoughts.

While there are different forms of CBT, including dialectic behavior therapy, rational living therapy, rational emotive behavior therapy, cognitive therapy, and rational behavior therapy, they all focus on similar core principles, including functional analysis, behavior modification, and skill training.

Functional analysis involves having the client and the therapist work together to explore the client's own thoughts and beliefs and the role they play in behavior. Clients are encouraged to talk openly and honestly about their substance use and explore the how drugs or alcohol have impacted their lives. Using techniques such as the *Socratic method*, clients learn to identify destructive beliefs and thinking patterns by questioning many of the assumptions they have always taken for granted in the past.

In the early stages of treatment, clients use functional analysis to understand the kind of triggers that can lead to risky behavior such as drug and alcohol abuse. They also gain insights into why they started abusing substances in the first place and the kind of high-risk situations that can lead to substance use. To help this process along, people in therapy are encouraged to keep a cognitive diary in which they record any thoughts or challenges they may have when not in treatment. Diaries are also useful in monitoring their behavior when they are in situations that might have led to substance use in the past (e.g., parties or other social gatherings).

Along with functional analysis, clients receive skill training to unlearn destructive habits and thought patterns and develop healthier alternatives. Using techniques such as cognitive restructuring, substance abusers learn to examine and change the addictive beliefs and automatic thinking patterns that can lead to habitual addiction-seeking behaviors. Addictive beliefs or automatic thinking patterns can include "I need my daily fix to socialize with other people," "I am powerless to control my cravings," or "drugs or alcohol will solve all my problems."

Along with reinforcing substance use, these automatic beliefs may reflect how users view themselves or the world in general. Having a poor opinion of their own self-worth, their current circumstances, or their family situation can also feed into the need to get high, not to mention helping to sabotage any attempt at ending the substance use. These beliefs also grow and change over time as users become increasingly pessimistic about the possibility of making a real change.

Automatic beliefs are often based on cognitive distortions or errors in thinking people often make. These include *all or nothing thinking* (seeing situations in black or white terms), *overgeneralizations* (viewing any setback as a sign that change is impossible), *mental filtering* to focus only on the negative, or *jumping to conclusions* about the way they view the world.

As part of their skill training, clients are taught how to incorporate these positive thought patterns into their daily life and to develop positive behavior patterns that can defeat the old patterns that encourage substance use. CBT can also be combined with relapse prevention therapy to help addicts identify what can lead them to relapse and to develop better coping strategies that don't require drug or alcohol use.

Over the course of treatment, clients can also engage in role play and behavioral rehearsal to learn more positive ways of thinking and behaving in situations that might lead to substance use. This also allows them to practice their new skills and become more comfortable in making them part of their daily routine. Other skills that can be learned during CBT sessions can include relaxation training, problem-solving training, stress inoculation, guided imagery, assertiveness training, and mindfulness training (more on that in Question 46).

Behavior modification (also known as contingency management) focuses on making positive changes in how a client behaves on a daily basis. This is often based on principles of operant conditioning by using specific rewards to reinforce positive behavior (such as remaining drug or alcohol free for a specific number of days). Different kinds of rewards can be used, including gift vouchers, spending time with friends or family, or some other form of recognition that can make staying sober more pleasurable. This allows clients attending treatment to make real changes to their daily routines that can continue long after the treatment program has ended.

Though designed to be a short-term treatment approach, CBT is time limited (having a fixed ending date after a set number of treatment sessions). As a result, clients are encouraged to plan how they will apply what they have learned once the treatment has ended. This makes CBT quite different from more traditional approaches such as twelve-step programs which are more open ended.

Research studies have demonstrated the effectiveness of CBT in the treatment of substance abuse, depression, eating disorders, and other mental health problems. Large-scale studies of CBT in the treatment of drug and alcohol use have found it to be especially beneficial in the treatment of cannabis, cocaine, and opioid addictions, with many clients found to be drug free for at least 12 months after the end of treatment. Combining CBT with other treatment approaches such as relapse prevention can be particularly useful in steering clients toward a healthier lifestyle.

46. What is mindfulness therapy?

Originally a part of Buddhist teachings, mindfulness deals with the process of focusing attention on the here and now without worrying about past experiences or fears about the future. Among the different mindfulness-based treatment approaches available are mindfulness-based cognitive therapy, mindfulness-based stress reduction, mindfulness-based substance abuse treatment for adolescents, and mindful-oriented recovery enhancement. For that matter, a growing number of "third-wave" behavioral treatments have included mindfulness training as modules used in their programs. These include acceptance and commitment therapy and dialectical behavior therapy.

Despite the numerous different approaches using mindfulness training, they all involve the use of meditation, guided imagery, or mental visualization exercises to allow people to focus on those specific thoughts, physical sensations, and desires that might be undermining their mental or physical health. This means that participants can learn how to take in and accept all incoming thoughts and feelings without resorting to automatic thoughts and beliefs that might be destructive. Also, much like with CBT, participants are given regular homework assignments so that they can regularly practice what they learn in the treatment sessions. This allows them to become more comfortable with the techniques as well as to use them on a daily basis.

Now widely used in the treatment of a range of mental health issues such as depression, stress, and social anxiety, mindfulness training represents one of the most promising approaches to helping addicts deal with cravings and withdrawal effects.

For people dealing with substance abuse, mindfulness training can be especially useful in accepting negative emotions and the physical cravings that can lead to relapse. Since people have an innate need to avoid painful situations and seek out pleasurable sensations, dealing with cravings is a perpetual problem for substance abusers who might otherwise want to stay clean.

One particular program developed by University of Washington researcher Sarah Bowen is known as *mindfulness-based relapse prevention*

(MBRP) and combines mindfulness training exercises such as meditation with standard relapse prevention programs. According to Bowen and her colleagues, substance abusers going through treatment are often encouraged to ignore cravings and avoid the different triggers that might lead to relapse. Instead, MBRP training encourages people dealing with substance abuse to acknowledge these cravings and triggers and to form their own choices about how to respond to them. By learning how to accept the craving and stress that can lead to relapse, substance abusers can disengage from their old automatic thoughts and behaviors and develop more positive alternatives.

Research looking at the effectiveness of mindfulness-based substance abuse treatment has shown that it can be especially beneficial in reducing cravings for a wide range of different addictive substances. This includes cravings for alcohol, amphetamines, tobacco, cocaine, marijuana, and opioids. Researchers examining the effects of mindfulness meditation on brain functioning have found evidence of significantly increased activity in the prefrontal cortex during meditation. Since this region of the brain has been linked to the nucleus accumbens and ventral tegmental area (both parts of the brain's central reward circuit), these research results suggest that mindfulness meditation can help boost the capacity for self-control. This could mean that mindfulness can make addicts better able to delay gratification and avoid relapsing.

One of the advantages of mindfulness training is the way that it can be combined with other group and individual treatment approaches and even included as part of family or couple therapy. Though there are some programs that it won't work well with (e.g., twelve-step programs), mindfulness-based training has become extremely popular among substance abuse counselors and their clients.

47. What can parents do to help children who are substance abusers?

While many adolescents or young adults with substance abuse problems may prefer to hide this from their parents and other family members for as long as possible, their substance use will come out sooner or later (see Questions 4 and 5 for some of the symptoms that may indicate substance use). Once this does come out however, parents often feel overwhelmed trying to come to terms with what has been happening right under their noses. Along with natural feelings of denial and anger, they often experience guilt as well over their perceived failure as parents. This is why parents of substance abusers often require counseling themselves to help guide them in what to do next to help their child.

Though they may find it difficult, it is essential that parents learn to accept that their child has a drug or alcohol problem. Just as important, it is also necessary to avoid making judgments about why their child is a substance abuser. There can be enormous temptation for parents to try playing the "blame game" and assuming that the abuse is occurring due to the influence of friends or acquaintances. Also, many parents may have their own beliefs about substance abuse as being something that doesn't happen in "good" families.

For this reason, the first step in coming to terms with their child's substance abuse problem is for parents to educate themselves about drug and alcohol abuse. Many of the books listed in the Directory of Resources can be helpful, but there are also numerous online and local resources that parents can use to find out more about the particular drugs their children have been using as well as the different treatment options available, preferably something in which parents can take part.

By working with addictions counselors and, if necessary, participating in support groups for parents of substance abusers, parents can often learn about the different treatment options available for their children and how to take an active role in that treatment. Depending on the nature of the substance abuse as well as many of the other emotional issues that addicts may be dealing with, parents and other family members may consider attending family counseling sessions with their children as part of the substance abuse treatment process.

One of the advantages of family counseling is its flexibility. Not only can counseling sessions be conducted individually or in groups, but they can also be used in conjunction with other forms of treatment that substance abusers may also need. Among the different goals of family counseling is to improve communications in the family, something that is often important considering the strain that can result from children keeping secrets from their parents (i.e., that they are using drugs or alcohol). Along with restoring communications, family therapy can help family members learn to trust one another and to address misunderstandings and long-term issues that they may never have been able to discuss openly. If there are other issues such as childhood physical or sexual abuse (which a parent may genuinely not know about) or if a child is coming to terms with issues surrounding sexual orientation, these can be explored in counseling sessions as well.

Even when their children have successfully completed treatment, parents need to take an active role to ensure their children stay clean, especially given the pressures they may face whenever they are in a social situation. For many adolescent substance abusers, the primary source of the drugs or alcohol they use will be their own friends, acquaintances, or even an older sibling. Parents need to stay vigilant and set a positive example that their children can follow. Warning children about the dangers of drugs or alcohol will be far more effective when parents abide by the same guidelines they set for their children, including abstaining from alcohol, tobacco, or other addictive substances.

Though many parents may feel that they have little real influence over their child's drug or alcohol use as they grow older and become more independent, they can still play an important role in how their children live their lives. Providing children who abuse substances with the emotional support they need can be an essential part of the treatment process.

48. Do online support groups help prevent future substance abuse?

For many substance abusers who want to attend treatment, the problem of finding treatment programs can be difficult, especially if they live in a smaller community where certain programs may not be available. Substance users attending treatment for the first time may also feel reluctant to become part of a treatment group where they would be expected to talk about their substance use and share many of their most intimate secrets with people they have never met before.

As a result, many substance users may be tempted to go online and take advantage of one of the numerous Internet support groups already available. Not only would this allow them to stay anonymous, but these groups are usually free and can be accessed at any time of the day or night.

But how effective are these online groups when compared to in-person treatment programs when it comes to avoiding any relapses? A recent research study examined a group of substance abusers who used both types of treatment groups and who had been in recovery for at least a year. Overall, participants who primarily attended face-to-face meetings had much more success in staying sober than those who primarily used online treatment programs.

One potential explanation for these results was provided by the study participants themselves, who admitted that they were much more likely to be open and honest when sharing at in-person meetings than they would online. Many people who abuse drugs or alcohol often have difficulty with honesty since lying makes it easier to hide their substance use, avoid being hassled by friends or family, and avoid being arrested. The longer they abuse substances, the easier the lying becomes. Since online groups often allow people to participate without revealing their identity, this removes much of the emotional connection that those participating in face-to-face meetings would experience. Meeting in person also allows substance abusers to relearn how to communicate honestly and avoid the impulse to lie when being asked uncomfortable questions. This also means not forming the kind of emotional bond that in-person group members often make, something that can be extremely important for people who want to open up about secrets they might not otherwise share.

Despite the disadvantages of online treatment programs, there is no disputing that they are becoming much more popular. Not only are there far more options available online that most people are likely to find in their own community, but joining an online group is far easier than finding an in-person treatment program. Considering that many programs may not be covered by standard health plans or receive government support, that also adds to the appeal of online treatment.

Though online treatment will continue to be popular, in-person treatment will continue to be available for people who need something more comprehensive to overcome addiction. Substance abusers seeking treatment should be able to investigate a wide range of treatment options. This can mean using online resources can be useful in supplementing the help that can come from conventional treatment though it should never replace it completely.

49. Does the risk of backsliding ever go away?

This is a question that every drug or alcohol abuser who has successfully completed treatment is going to ask sooner or later. Unfortunately, the risk of relapsing will always be there though staying clean will become easier with time. As substance users develop healthier habits and better ways of coping with stress and cravings, the temptation to use will slowly subside as well.

Still, there are always going to be danger signs that users will need to watch out for to ensure they avoid relapsing. Many of these danger signs were already discussed in Question 42 when we learned about the different stages of relapsing, including *emotional relapse*, *mental relapse*, and *physical relapse*. Recovering substance users need to be especially careful in watching for any signs of emotional or mental relapse, especially if they are dealing with significant stress or a major life crisis.

This means watching for signs of emotional distress since this can frequently catch substance users off guard. As a result, they may not realize they are letting things get out of control until too late. This means watching for feelings of being "on edge" and more depressed or angry, or lying awake at night because of worry. By allowing these feelings to go unchecked for too long, *mental relapse* can often occur.

In mental relapse, thoughts about using drugs or alcohol again become more frequent and increasingly harder to deal with. Given the biological roots of substance abuse, spending too much time in the mental relapse stage can lead to the addiction centers of the brain becoming more active. As a result, users can become more aware of renewed cravings and increased awareness of the old triggers that can lead to substance use.

Users experiencing mental relapse can also begin sabotaging their efforts to stay sober, often by putting themselves in risky situations where substance use becomes more likely. This is where *apparently irrelevant decisions* can come into play. No matter how confident they might feel about not falling back into the same old trap, users in danger of relapse can still find themselves taking a new route home from work or school that *happens* to pass by a bar or some other place where drugs can be easily purchased.

After emotional and mental relapse comes physical relapse and a return to drug or alcohol use. For many users, this can often become a reason for despair and the feeling that any attempt at staying clean will be doomed to failure. Admitting to friends and family that they have relapsed despite their treatment can mean shame or guilt at letting the people in their lives down and that they will have to do treatment all over again.

Still, as time passes without a relapse and substance abusers learn to live their lives without drugs or alcohol, the risk of relapsing does diminish. Unfortunately, the danger of overconfidence is something to watch out for, even with people who believe themselves "cured" of addiction. More on that is discussed in the next question.

50. Can substance abusers learn to move on with their lives?

For substance abusers who have successfully completed treatment and have remained drug and alcohol free for a while, the key to really move on with life rests in the kind of positive habits they develop that take the place of the old, harmful habits. These harmful habits can include using drugs or alcohol to be social or to cope with stress, as well as the different situational triggers leading to substance use.

But habits, once formed, can be remarkably difficult to change. According to the English poet John Dryden, "We first make our habits and then our habits make us." For people who develop substance abuse habits due to early childhood problem or abuse especially, overcoming those habits and substituting them with healthier ones can be long and difficult, but with time, it does become possible. As we've seen in the sections on relapse prevention and cognitive behavioral therapy, part of the process underlying treatment is to challenge the unhealthy habits that reinforce substance use and replace them with healthier habits that can help abusers stay clean.

Whatever form these new healthy habits take, whether by healthy nutrition, exercise, or relying on stress management techniques to help cope with the inevitable hassles of life, they need time and practice to become deeply ingrained. Still, once they are ingrained, they become second nature to us, and sticking to this new lifestyle becomes easier.

For former substance users, living without drugs or alcohol often means a clean break with acquaintances and places that might otherwise lead to a return to old habits. This can mean completely changing what they might do in their free time, the things they do to cope with stress, and the various situational triggers that once led to getting high. Though people in recovery may be conflicted about making such fundamental changes, especially if it means distancing themselves from longtime acquaintances who are still using, developing these new habits is essential to make a true recovery.

Granted, it takes time to build a new support network made up of friends who will help former users stay clean. Many treatment programs and twelve-step groups can provide advice and encouragement to help this process along. It's also important to rely on family members and close friends who can provide needed emotional support while people in recovery turn their lives around. Sadly, this can often be difficult for substance users who feel uncomfortable turning to these same people they've let down before. If this is a problem, family or couples counseling can help overcome the old barriers and enable recovering substance abusers and their families to move on with their lives.

Though the risk of relapse will always be there, learning to recognize the warning signs (see previous question) and taking the necessary actions to prevent relapses will become easier with time. That also means sticking with the positive health habits and, for many recovering users, taking an active role in helping other substance abusers learn to turn their own lives around. This can mean becoming a twelve-steps sponsor or doing volunteer work for one of the many organizations available for helping addicts get clean. Not only does this allow recovering addicts to "pay it forward," but also this allows to reinforce what they have learned in treatment.

As for the question of whether substance abusers can learn to move on with their lives, the answer is a definite "yes" though this can be a long and difficult road to follow. While relapses can and do occur, it is still possible to build a new life without drugs or alcohol. All it takes is for recovering users to learn what they did wrong in relapsing and get back on the path to recovery. So long as they aren't willing to give up, nothing will stop them from succeeding.

Case Studies

CASE 1: WAYNE

Wayne is a 45-year-old factory worker whose problems with substance abuse began after a car accident left him with severe back and shoulder pain. Despite physiotherapy and massage, the pain showed little improvement, and Wayne grew frustrated due to his inability to work or do any of the hobbies he used to enjoy. While his doctor prescribed OxyContin for pain, Wayne became upset since the prescribed dosage wasn't helping and his doctor refused to prescribe anything stronger. Since his wife had some morphine remaining from a previous shoulder injury, Wayne decided to take these pills along with the medication prescribed by his doctor.

While the morphine helped with the pain, Wayne soon discovered that his tolerance was increasing and he was soon taking more of the pills to keep his pain under control. Though he tried "double dipping" by going to another doctor to get more pain medication, his original doctor became aware of what was happening and warned his colleague.

Though his doctor confronted Wayne about his misusing prescription drugs, Wayne refused to admit the possibility that he might have a problem with substance abuse. As he pointed out to his doctor, his only real problem was his pain and not getting the medication he needed to keep it under control. He was also pessimistic about whether his pain would ever go away on its own. Though his doctor offered to refer his patient to an addiction specialist, Wayne decided to try another doctor who might be more sympathetic.

Though he went to different doctors, Wayne's chronic medication-seeking, as well as the concerns raised by his previous doctors, meant that no reputable physician was willing to prescribe him medication. He also found that trying to go off the medication, either cold turkey or through gradual tapering, led to problems, including diarrhea, nausea, bodily aches, and a powerful craving that he couldn't handle for long. Finally, after months of getting medication any way that he could, he began buying his drugs illegally, including known drug dealers, often at great expense. After many lucky escapes, Wayne was eventually caught purchasing medication illegally from an Internet site that was being monitored by the Drug Enforcement Agency and he was charged.

Given his lack of a previous criminal history, Wayne received a suspended sentence with the condition that he seek treatment for his prescription drug abuse. While he grudgingly admitted that he had a problem during the weekly sessions with an addictions counselor that had been ordered by the court, Wayne continued to insist that his chronic pain was the main cause for his drug use. He also insisted he still needed stronger medication than any physician was willing to give him because of addiction concerns. Due to his anger over his legal problems, as well as his low self-esteem over being unable to work, Wayne was placed on antidepressant medication that helped him get his mood problems under control.

The first stage of Wayne's treatment involved a complete drug detox with physical symptoms and mental discomfort that lasted for weeks. Recognizing the impact that his withdrawal was having on him, Wayne's doctor referred him to a local methadone clinic where he received a weekly dose specifically tailored to him according to his body weight and history of opiate abuse. Considering his pain issues, the methadone was administered in conjunction with non-opiate pain relievers.

In addition to his methadone dose, he attended regular sessions with an addictions counselor at the clinic. Due to her own concerns about Wayne's drug use, Wayne's wife arranged to attend sessions along with him to help him come to terms with his drug use.

During these weekly treatment sessions, Wayne learned about the physical and psychological dependence problems that often come with pain medication, especially opiate-based medications. He also came to acknowledge that he had allowed his pain medication use to get out of control, hence his legal situation. Also, while his pain was still a significant problem, he learned more effective ways of dealing with pain, including stress management and mindfulness techniques and multidisciplinary pain treatment at a pain clinic. His doctor also prescribed non-opiate-based pain medication though it needed to be carefully monitored to prevent overuse.

While his sessions are still ongoing, Wayne has developed greater confidence that he can get his addiction issues under control and is in the process of tapering off the methadone under medical supervision. Although he recognizes that the process is a long one, he and his wife are more hopeful about the future.

Analysis

For chronic pain patients and their doctors, finding the right dosage to provide effective pain relief while reducing the risk of drug dependence can be tricky. Since many pain medications are opiate based, long-term use often leads to increased drug tolerance (requiring more of the medication to get the same benefit) as well as withdrawal effects when the medication is stopped for any reason. Withdrawal effects in themselves are not a sign of addiction but simply a normal consequence of prolonged medication use. Still, some pain patients may find themselves becoming alarmed by the possibility of withdrawal and suffer needlessly as a result. Also, many pain patients may not recognize the potential danger of misusing prescription pain medications, whether they consider themselves incapable of becoming addicted or because they refuse to recognize the addictive potential of many popular medications. For patients like Wayne, warning signs that medication use is out of control include raising the dosage without medical approval, attempting to get medication from other doctors, or taking medication without a medical prescription. This means that disposing of unused pain medication is something that needs to be done as quickly and safely as possible to prevent others from taking it accidentally or on purpose. Instructions for safe disposal of prescription medication can be found online or in consumer guides.

CASE 2: MARY

Mary was never much of a drinker before she went to college. If anything, she had a reputation in high school of being too restrained and often avoided parties where drugs or alcohol would be used. Her parents were extremely strict, and she was well aware how they would have responded at any suggestion that their daughter was "out of control." Part of the reason she chose to attend college in another city was to become more independent and make her own choices.

Once she began college and was living in a dormitory on campus, alcohol seemed to be everywhere and she decided that she was mature enough to handle it on her own. She also became more involved in socializing with the students who had become her new friends, and many of them were attending the kind of parties that she had avoided in the past. Though she was extremely careful about how much alcohol she consumed at these parties, people always seemed to be pressuring her to drink more and, at times, she would give in to this pressure.

Unfortunately, all the opportunities to socialize began cutting into her study time, and she found herself falling behind in several of her classes. She also had difficulty coping with her class schedule, managing her limited finances, and going on dates whenever possible. Worrying about her grades and the upcoming course schedule also meant that she had trouble sleeping at night, something that made it even harder to keep up with her schoolwork.

Mary soon found herself drinking more frequently as a way of coping with the stress and also as a way of controlling social anxiety whenever she was at parties. Though several of her friends expressed concern about her drinking, Mary insisted that she had it under control. She became more secretive about how much she was drinking, including buying alcohol to drink in her own room: a clear violation of dormitory rules.

While she managed to conceal her alcohol use from her professors, coming into early morning class while dealing with a hangover became a regular experience for her. Again, friends told her how worried they were becoming, and Mary often became openly hostile toward them.

After she was caught drinking in the dormitory and warned about possible academic suspension if it happened again, Mary began looking into moving off campus where she could be more open about her alcohol use. Considering her limited finances, she had few real options and restricted her drinking to the various student pubs around campus.

It was only after nearly being sexually assaulted at a bar off campus that Mary began to recognize that her drinking was out of control. By this time however, she found that cutting herself off completely led to a range of unpleasant symptoms, including nausea, sweating, heart palpitations, and headaches. Though she didn't link these symptoms to her drinking at first, a school nurse she consulted explained that what she was experiencing tended to be common for heavy drinkers who stopped suddenly. This, more than anything else, brought home to her how much of a problem she really had.

Frightened of the potential impact that her alcoholism could have on her academic career, not to mention how her parents would react,

Mary went to the university's counseling center to talk to one of the peer counselors. She was initially afraid of how confidential such a talk would be, but after meeting the counselor she would be working with, Gwen, and the faculty member who was supervising her, Mary decided to take a chance and told them both her story.

Both Gwen and her supervisor, Dr. Farley, reassured Mary that she was doing the right thing by seeking treatment and that admitting to having a problem was a vital first step. Substance abuse is a major problem on campus, and Mary was given the option of individual sessions with Gwen or joining one of the substance abuse treatment groups that were already running at the center. Mary admitted to being nervous about speaking about her drinking in a group, and her individual sessions began right away.

Through these sessions, Mary learned more about how common it was for young adults away from home for the first time to become overwhelmed by all the freedom that came with it, including the freedom to drink. Working with Gwen, she developed a practical plan that would involve carefully monitoring her exposure to alcohol, including the drinking that went on at all the parties she attended, and to recognize the cues that triggered her own drinking behavior. While her treatment has just begun, she and Gwen remain hopeful.

Analysis

For many adolescents and young adults who are out on their own for the first time in their lives, the greater freedom they experience carries risks as well. While alcohol is fine in moderation, everybody has a realistic limit, and young people like Mary may not have the experience to recognize when that limit has been reached. There are other dangers as well, especially in college settings where women who have had too much to drink may be targeted by males at parties. According to some estimates, as many as 15 percent of all women in their freshman year may experience date rape while incapacitated on alcohol or drugs, something Mary had been fortunate to avoid. Though many colleges have been trying to provide better safeguards to prevent these assaults from occurring, the easy availability of drugs and alcohol on most campuses makes this problematic. An estimated four out of five of all college students admit to drinking or using drugs, and half of those who do use also admit to binge drinking or drug use. Also, many college students who drink or use drugs may have been doing so since they were adolescents, making their substance abuse much harder to treat. While drug and alcohol treatment programs are available, students such as Mary are often faced with the challenge of staying the course considering the constant temptations that occur whenever they get together socially. Unfortunately, it can be extremely difficult for them to recognize that their substance use is out of control and that they need help. Until they do, the problem is only going to get worse.

CASE 3: GREGORY

Gregory is a 14-year-old honor student enrolled in an exclusive preparatory school. The pressure for him to succeed academically is intense, and he is feeling the strain of keeping up with all of his coursework. As it happens, he knows someone his age, "Barry," who happens to be a friend of his cousin. Barry was diagnosed with attention deficit hyperactivity disorder (ADHD) years before and had been placed on Ritalin. Barry didn't like the side effects the medication was causing and had slowly cut back the dosage without telling anyone else, including his doctor. This gives him a fair supply of the medication that he has been quietly selling to other kids his age who want "pep pills" to help with schoolwork. After approaching Barry, Gregory soon became his best customer, and he found that the Ritalin tablets worked well in helping him stay focused. He had researched stimulants on the Internet and felt that he could handle any problems that might arise, something that even Barry had warned him about.

Problems soon developed when Gregory realized that he was developing a tolerance for Ritalin, and he began taking increasingly more to get the same benefit. While there had been several minor "crashes," he had usually been able to hide this from his teachers and family (though his friends soon realized something was wrong). With the increased Ritalin dosage however, Gregory soon reached a point where his drug usage had become much more dangerous. Finally, after a severe crash, complete with convulsions, hallucinations, and severe neurological pain, his parents finally realized what was happening and became alarmed.

Though Gregory viewed his parents' discovery as a catastrophe, it probably saved his life or, at the very least, prevented his drug use from seriously damaging his health. For his parents, Andrew and Beth, the revelation that their only son had been abusing stimulants for months was hard to accept though they had their own experiences with substance abuse in the past. Beth's father had been an alcoholic and Andrew's brother had been through drug rehabilitation himself, something that they had kept from Gregory for years given how shameful they felt this to be. Still, they were realistic enough to know that simply ordering Gregory to stop wouldn't be enough. After consulting with their family doctor, who referred them to a specialist in adolescent substance abuse, Gregory and his parents began attending family counseling together.

Though Gregory had become upset when his parents withdrew him from school pending completion of his drug treatment program, he eventually recognized that his health was more important. As for the school administrators, they agreed to allow Gregory to remain as a student and that no charges would be laid in his case as long as he agreed to cooperate. Andrew and Beth also notified Barry's parents and warned them that they would lay a complaint if he attempted to sell his medication in future. This ended any chance of Gregory buying medicine from Barry again though his parents knew that he could find stimulants elsewhere if he were motivated enough.

During his treatment sessions, Gregory learned more about how amphetamines can affect the brain and what prolonged use can do to the brain and central nervous system. He also learned about better ways of handling academic stress and how to manage his time more effectively. Since he had always been a good student, it was important that he overcome the self-doubt that led him to rely on stimulants in the first place. Gregory also came to recognize that the extremely high expectations that he had for himself did more harm than good, something that his parents needed to accept as well.

After the treatment sessions ended, Gregory decided to return to the same school, but he also reduced his course load with fewer advanced placement courses to make his schoolwork more manageable. He still maintained his high grades, but much of the pressure that he had placed on himself had been relieved. Also, his early experience with stimulants made him less willing to experiment with other drugs or alcohol in future. On his own initiative, he decided to continue seeing the drug counselor on a semi-regular basis to reinforce what he had learned during his treatment program. While his parents were less willing to recognize that their son was still vulnerable, they encouraged him to continue. By remaining part of his drug treatment, they hoped that he would be more willing to open up to them if any future problems developed.

Analysis

While medications such as Adderall and Ritalin are primarily used for treating ADHD, they have also gained a reputation as "study drugs" used by high school and university students seeking to boost their grades. Not only do stimulants allow students to function with less sleep, but they often report being able to concentrate more effectively. Considering the pressure many students face to excel, the temptation to use cognitive enhancing drugs can be overwhelming. But there are drawbacks to using stimulant medication as a quick fix instead of developing better study habits. Not only does the body build up greater tolerance over time so that a higher dosage is needed to get the same effect, but the long-term effects of stimulant use in users without ADHD can be devastating. Some of the symptoms commonly reported in students abusing stimulants include irritability, suppressed appetite, insomnia, and anxiety. In extreme cases, stimulant users can report "crashing" due to loss of sleep, dehydration/ malnutrition, physical exhaustion, and mental hyperactivity. This can lead to a sense of being "tired and wired" when racing thoughts make sleep impossible no matter how exhausted students may feel.

What makes fighting stimulant abuse so difficult is that students often think of these drugs as harmless since they aren't really seen as addictive and can be purchased legally in many places. Also, contrary to belief, research has shown that overuse of stimulants can lead to poorer academic performance since many students may become less engaged in class as a result. Many schools have introduced programs to educate students about the dangers of stimulant use and encourage "natural studying" though drug educators admit that much work still remains to be done.

CASE 4: SUSAN

Susan is a 23-year-old heroin addict whose history of using dates back to her late teens. Though she has made previous attempts to quit, she has rarely been able to stay clean for long. While she has experimented with other drugs, including alcohol, heroin remains her drug of choice, and she is able to function reasonably well so long as she is able to avoid issues with drug withdrawal. Many of her friends are also drug users, and she has isolated herself from family or friends who tried pressuring her to quit in the past. She is involved in an abusive relationship with Mark, who is also a heroin user with a history of frequent brushes with the law. Mark is her primary drug supplier, though she is aware of other sources who can provide her heroin if she needs it.

Despite her drug habit, Susan has managed to avoid health problems relating to unsafe drug practices and also gets regular medical check-ups (though her doctor is unaware of her drug use). At her most recent appointment, Susan learned that she is pregnant, something that she had not expected. This pregnancy sparked a new crisis for her, one for which Mark and her remaining friends provided little real support. She decided to continue with the pregnancy though Mark refused any responsibility for the child, and she also recognized that she would need to end all drug use for the sake of her pregnancy.

The problem for Susan was that she had never been able to abstain from heroin for longer than a few months, making her uncertain whether she could last until giving birth. She also received contradictory advice from different friends, some of whom assured her that the medical risks of using heroin while pregnant are exaggerated and the stress of going without heroin would cause even more problems while pregnant.

When Susan presented herself at an addiction clinic, she had a full examination to rule out any potential infections from intravenous drug use. But she also faced legal challenges, including dealing with a child care worker who was assigned to her case. As the worker made clear to her, she would likely face criminal charges if she took any drugs while pregnant.

Susan was also warned about the risks that suddenly stopping her heroin use could have on her unborn baby. The withdrawal caused by suddenly stopping all heroin use can lead to severe medical problems, including seizures, tachycardia (rapid heartbeat), nausea, vomiting, diarrhea, insomnia, and tremors. In many cases, these symptoms can be so severe that users often relapse due to the traumatic effects of withdrawal. As for her baby, quitting heroin cold turkey could also mean an increased risk of miscarriage or birth defects.

Given her circumstances, the doctors at the clinic decided to place Susan in a methadone maintenance program until she gave birth. As the only medically approved treatment for opiate-dependent pregnant women in the United States, Susan had no other real option if she wished to deliver her baby safely. Though the baby would likely be born with a methadone dependence, detox is safe and effective while carried out under proper medical supervision. There are other medical concerns associated with methadone use during pregnancy, including low birth weight and smaller-than-normal head size though babies usually develop normally as they grow older.

In addition to her methadone treatment, Susan's case was monitored by a clinic social worker as well as a case worker from child protection services. She also attended weekly group and individual counseling sessions and, given the end of her relationship with Mark, was encouraged to contact her parents for help, something she was reluctant to do at first. With the aid of her social worker, who sat in on her first meeting with her parents in three years, she has managed a reconciliation and has agreed to move back home until giving birth. Her social worker encouraged this plan since it would mean continuing support as well as putting distance between Susan and her drug-using friends, including Mark.

While Susan is functioning well with her current treatment, she knows that she has tough choices to make about what she wishes to do after the baby is born. Given that she will be under the constant supervision of child protection services if she decides to raise the child herself, she would need to commit herself to remaining on the methadone program and continue with drug addiction counseling.

Analysis

Among the various medical issues surrounding drug and alcohol abuse, the potential dangers faced by pregnant women remain one of the most critical. Though most of the research literature dealing with substance abuse during pregnancy focuses on alcohol use, there is a growing awareness of how drug use can affect prenatal development and lead to a range of medicals problems. These problems include miscarriage, stillbirth, premature birth, low birth weight, and cognitive impairments. Specific drugs are known to have adverse prenatal effects, including heroin, cocaine, inhalants, marijuana, amphetamines, nicotine, and certain over-the-counter and prescription drugs. This is why all women need to be careful about potential exposure to substances that might harm their babies, whether during pregnancy or while breastfeeding.

Babies of mothers who abuse substances also run the risk of being born dependent on whatever drug the mother was taking during pregnancy—a condition known as neonatal abstinence syndrome. How severe the withdrawal effects are for newborns often depends on the type of drug used, how often the birth mother abused drugs during pregnancy, how the body breaks down the drug, and whether or not the baby was born prematurely or full term. Withdrawal symptoms can include seizures, rapid breathing or heart rate, slow weight gain, sleep problems, or sweating. Even with careful treatment, the consequences of withdrawal in infant can be severe.

At the present time, methadone maintenance treatment remains the gold standard for pregnant women addicted to opioids such as heroin. Though friends and family often advise drug abusers who are pregnant to stop drug use completely, methadone therapy should only be discontinued after seeking medical advice.

CASE 5: TIM

Tim is a 17-year-old young offender currently serving a sentence in a youth reformatory. Given his long history of juvenile offenses, including property and drug charges, the judge warned him at his latest sentencing that he would be tried as an adult the next time he appeared in court. He was also ordered to attend drug and alcohol counseling while inside and to continue with treatment when he returns to the community.

While Tim remained open to attending addictions counseling, he has been in a number of programs before and always seemed to return to his regular drug and alcohol use sooner or later. As he told the drug counselor at his first session, he had been using drugs and alcohol since he was 11 years old, though his most serious abuse didn't begin until his early teens. Both of his parents were addicts, and while his mother had tried to insulate Tim as much as possible, his father was physically abusive and often either drunk or stoned (he would later die of an overdose when Tim was 13). Given this early exposure to drugs and abuse, it isn't surprising that both of Tim's siblings have also gotten in trouble with the law although Tim has the longest record of the three.

After being removed from the family home when he was 12, Tim went through a number of different foster homes and group homes, but his frequent brushes with the law meant that he rarely stayed long. This also meant that his education has been fairly limited, and testing revealed that he reads at a grade five level.

When asked about his drug and alcohol use, he described a regular pattern of abuse, including stealing to get the money he needed to support his habit. While he has tried numerous different drugs, including mixing drugs and alcohol, his drug of choice has always been crack cocaine, which he uses regularly when in the community and has even managed to buy some while inside on several occasions. Virtually all of his offenses either were related to drugs directly or involved property crimes committed to raise money for drugs.

While Tim has been careful not to ally himself with any of the known gang members who were doing time along with him, most of his friends on the inside are also drug users, and they often exchange tips on places to get drugs on the outside as well as possible "scores" that can bring in money, whether inside or out in the community. Tim recognizes that he is well on the way to becoming a career criminal and admits to wanting to straighten out his life though this seems unlikely as long as he continues to use drugs. He also worries about his two younger siblings and hopes to keep them away from drugs if possible.

During the course of his treatment sessions with the drug counselor, Tim placed much of the blame for his drug addiction and his criminal history on his father and often minimized his own responsibility for the choices he made in his life. In talking about his father's addiction, including the intravenous drug use that led to his developing hepatitis C (which he passed on to Tim's mother), Tim insisted that he had no real choice except to be an addict like his father. Even as he discussed many of the positive influences in his family, including his grandparents, Tim had trouble accepting that he had made a conscious decision to start using drugs and alcohol and to start committing crimes to feed his habit.

Even when he acknowledged responsibility for his actions, he also insisted that he had no control over the urges that led him to relapse time and again. In describing several examples from his past, his counselor noted how Tim continued to put himself in situations where he faced temptation as well as associating with friends and acquaintances who were also substance abusers. As his counselor pointed out to him, the main reason for his relapsing was Tim's own tendency to sabotage himself every chance he could get. If he really wanted to end his substance abuse, he would need to make radical changes in how he would live his life after his release. This included staying away from the negative influences in his life and developing a positive support network on release.

To aid this plan, his counselor made arrangements for Tim to enter a halfway house for substance abusers even though they are often reluctant to accept ex-convicts due to their high recidivism rate. Though Tim says that he is motivated to end his drug and alcohol abuse, his case worker recognizes that he has a long upward battle ahead of him.

Analysis

Drug and alcohol abusers with a history of early substance use (typically before the age of puberty) are often considered to have a poor prognosis when it comes to quitting. Since this kind of early substance use is usually seen in young offenders with an extensive criminal history, not to mention long-term personality problems such as antisocial personality or borderline personality disorder, they can frequently sabotage their own efforts to stay clean due to impulsiveness or being immersed in a criminal lifestyle that makes rehabilitation even more problematic. With young offenders such as Tim, participating in substance abuse programs is only part of the process of becoming rehabilitated. Not only would he need vocational education and training to prepare him to function in society, but he would also need to separate himself completely from negative associates who might lead him to relapse.

Also, a relatively short-term program would likely not be enough considering how deeply rooted Tim's criminal lifestyle and substance abuse really were. Even after completing his program, he would likely still need follow-up counseling to help him maintain his drug- and alcohol-free lifestyle. Relapse prevention counseling, which has already been covered in this book, can help Tim spot the apparently irrelevant decisions that might sabotage him and also to learn how to handle the impulsiveness that has often gotten him into trouble in the past.

Fortunately for Tim and others like him, there are good resources available in the community that can help make the transition easier. Many of those resources are listed in the Directory of Resources.

Glossary

Alcohol-related dementia: A form of dementia caused by long-term, excessive drinking of alcoholic beverages, often resulting in significant brain damage and cognitive problems such as loss of memory, impaired motor functioning, psychosis, and language disorder.

Cognitive restructuring (CR): Therapeutic process used to identify and change irrational or maladaptive thought patterns; a key component for cognitive behavioral psychotherapy and rational-emotive behavior therapy. Studies have confirmed the effectiveness of CR in the treatment of problems such as addiction and depression.

Conduct disorder: A psychiatric diagnosis given to adolescents and pre-adolescents showing a repeated pattern of behavior problems. The two main forms of conduct disorders are *childhood-onset* conduct disorder, with conduct disorder symptoms developing before the age of 10, and *adolescent-onset* conduct disorder, with behavior problems developing at a later age. Chronic substance use is one of the main symptoms linked with this disorder.

Delirium tremens: A serious medical condition also known as the DTs; usually seen in chronic alcoholics who have developed a long-term tolerance to alcohol after their intake has been dramatically reduced or stopped. Symptoms for delirium tremens include rapid mental confusion, shaking, sweating, and, at times, visual hallucinations. Seizures and an abnormally high body temperature can also set in, which may be fatal if left untreated. Since the "half-life" for alcohol is relatively long, it usually takes several days after the last drink for delirium tremens to set in. Once the symptoms begin, they can last for three days or more and often require intensive hospital care to monitor for medical complications.

Dependence: An adaptive state that occurs due to repeated drug or alcohol use leading to out-of-control behavior that persists despite a desire to quit. Dependence can take the form of *psychological* or *physical dependence* as well as a combination of the two.

Designer drugs: Drugs designed to mimic controlled substances as a way of bypassing existing drug laws.

Detoxification: Also known as detox for short, this is the process of helping people overcome cravings and withdrawal effects through the abrupt termination of drugs or alcohol under medical supervision, usually on an inpatient basis. It is often the first step in treatment for people dealing with severe drug or alcohol abuse and a longtime pattern of substance use. This can occur on an either inpatient or outpatient basis depending on how severe the pattern of addiction is.

Drug literacy programs: Programs aimed at educating young people about drugs and alcohol to allow them to make responsible choices and avoid health problems that might otherwise arise.

Emotional relapse: The first stage of relapse in which users who once depended on drugs or alcohol to manage stress may find themselves dealing with a stressful situation that their substance-free lifestyle hasn't yet equipped them to handle. This can include feeling more "on edge," feeling more depressed or angry, or problems getting to sleep at night which users may not recognize until it is too late, which is followed by mental relapse.

Fetal alcohol spectrum disorder (FASD): A series of medical conditions that can occur due to prenatal exposure to alcohol. In its most extreme form, fetal alcohol syndrome is characterized by abnormal appearance, small head size, poor coordination, and cognitive and behavioral problems developing later in life. Even in relatively mild form, fetal alcohol exposure can result in premature birth, low birth weight, and learning problems.

Harm reduction: A term used for strategies intended to reduce the negative consequences associated with drug use. Principles of harm reduction include a reduced emphasis on criminal prosecution and recognition that drug use will continue regardless of legal consequences. Strategies can include establishment of safe injection sites, needle exchanges to reduce infection, education campaigns to increase awareness of drug and alcohol abuse, and better outreach services.

Mental relapse: Following a period of emotional relapse, mental relapse can set in, with thoughts about using drugs or alcohol again becoming more frequent and increasingly harder to deal with. This can mean renewed cravings and increased awareness of the old triggers that often led to substance use. People experiencing mental relapse can also begin sabotaging their efforts to stay sober, whether by skipping treatment sessions or putting themselves in risky situations where substance use becomes more likely. The next stage is physical relapse.

Methadone maintenance treatment: An often-controversial therapy using methadone to alleviate withdrawal effects in people addicted to heroin and other opioids. Since methadone can also be abused as a street drug, access is tightly controlled in most jurisdictions and medical doctors can prescribe it only after completing a specialized training program.

Mindfulness: The process of focusing attention on the present moment through the use of meditation and mental visualization exercises. Originally a part of Buddhist teachings, mindfulness training exercises are now widely used in the treatment of a range of mental health issues such as depression, stress, and social anxiety. Specific forms of therapy based on mindfulness training include dialectical behavior therapy, mode deactivation therapy, and mindfulness relaxation.

Minority stress theory: A potential explanation for increased substance use in sexual minorities. According to this theory, minorities experience unique stress issues stemming from the active discrimination and harassment they frequently face as well as internalized self-hatred. Such stress may result in increased mental health problems as well as issues such as substance abuse and suicide.

Naloxone: An anti-opioid agent that is often sold under the brand name of Narcan. Naloxone bonds to opioid receptors in the central nervous system allowing it to counteract the effects of most opioids rapidly. For this reason, it has become a standard treatment for all forms of opioid overdoses and is also becoming increasingly available in many pharmacies.

Negative parenting: Often taking the form of emotional neglect, lack of positive reinforcement, failing to set proper limits, or monitoring, this type of parenting is seen as being most likely to lead to later problems, including substance abuse in later life; contrasted with positive parenting.

Neonatal opiate analgesic dependence: A medical condition stemming from prenatal exposure to opioids. Along with birth complications, infants born opioid dependent often show problems such as diarrhea, irritability, sneezing, tremors, and chronic vomiting.

Physical relapse: Following emotional and mental relapse, physical relapse is the final stage during which a user actually returns to drug or alcohol use. Many users may see this as a sign that the addiction is too strong and any effort to stay clean is doomed to failure. With relapse prevention training however, any relapse is treated as a learning experience, which can be used to recognize how to avoid it from happening again in future.

Physiological dependence: Refers to the changes that occur in the body with chronic overuse of different kinds of psychoactive substances. As a result, the body becomes dependent on regular substance intake and often leads to problems with withdrawal and tolerance due to prolonged use. Among the substances linked to physiological dependence are alcohol; all types of opioids including heroin, morphine, and oxycodone; barbiturates; benzodiazepines; and many psychiatric medications.

Prolapse: The opposite of relapse in which a user turns away from destructive behaviors toward more positive and healthier behaviors; a common term used in relapse prevention training.

Psychogenic, or character defect theory of addiction: A largely discredited theory that lays the blame for addiction on the addict's inability to control his or her own innate impulses, leading to drug or alcohol addiction.

Psychological dependence: The formation of a psychological need for continued substance use due to the role it plays in coping and stress management. Withdrawal can take the form of motivation and emotional symptoms such as anxiety, depression, and a reduced ability to experience pleasure.

Relapse prevention (RP): A cognitive behavioral approach to substance abuse treatment focusing on the identification of high-risk situations that can increase the likelihood of relapsing. Relapse prevention training involves teaching addicts coping strategies that can help with craving and apparently irrelevant decisions that can lead to dangerous situations. Patients are also trained to manage behavioral lapses and to develop positive addictions that can counteract negative ones. Research has shown that RP has significant value in the treatment of drug and alcohol addiction and has also been adapted for dealing with compulsive behaviors, obesity, and depression.

Sensation-seeking: A psychological trait marked by openness to new experiences and a willingness to take risks. People high in sensation-seeking are prone to participating in activities such as "thrill-seeking," extreme sports, or illegal activities such as gambling or shoplifting. High sensation-seekers are also more likely to abuse stimulants, hallucinogens, or alcohol due to the "high" such drugs can bring and can quickly become dependent on them.

Social drinking: Casual drinking in a social environment without the intention of becoming intoxicated. While often referred to as "responsible drinking," social drinkers may still develop a pattern of dependence in which they require alcohol to enjoy social interaction.

Stepping-Stone Theory of Drug Abuse: A largely discredited theory suggesting that mild drugs such as cannabis *inevitably* lead to more severe drug abuse, as well as addiction to narcotics. Since convicted heroin or cocaine addicts often reported having used cannabis at some point, antidrug campaigners demanded that cannabis use be brought under control due to its "corrupting influence"; this theory has led to more modern theories, suggesting that "gateway drugs" can increase the risk of more severe drug addiction.

Substance abuse: Defined as overdependence on a psychoactive substance leading to a systematic pattern of dependence. Formerly referred to as "drug abuse," the term "substance abuse" has become more common since it includes psychoactive substances that are legal in many places, such as alcohol, caffeine, and tobacco.

Substance disorder: Refers to the cognitive, behavioral, and medical issues associated with abusing psychoactive substances; often confused with substance use disorders.

Substance-induced disorders: Refers to medical conditions that can result from chronic drug or alcohol use. Substance-induced disorders can include intoxication and withdrawal effects as well as many of the neurological and cognitive problems associated with them.

Substance use disorders: Another name for drug or alcohol addiction and is characterized by psychological or physical dependence on a psychoactive substance.

Tolerance: The diminished response to an addictive substance that occurs when the substance is used repeatedly. Tolerance usually develops as the body adapts to the regular substance, leading to larger and larger doses being required to achieve the same effect.

Toxicity: The degree to which a chemical substance or mixture of substances can seriously harm the body when taken. Toxicity can refer to how it affects the whole body or specific organs of the body and often depends on the dosage used as well as the chemical structure of the substance. While the primary danger in drug or alcohol use stems from the potential for overdose, many street drugs as well as alcohol from unknown sources may contain potentially toxic ingredients, which can lead to serious illness or death.

Treatment plan: A plan outlining the goals that need to be met and the type of treatment that might be needed to achieve those goals. Developed jointly by the patient and therapist, treatment plans provide short- and long-term goals for patients as well as methods for determining how the goals are met.

Twelve-step program: A recovery group based on the 12 principles and practices originally proposed by Bill Wilson in founding Alcoholics

Anonymous (AA). Described as a program of recovery, the 12 steps involve recognition that the substance use is out of control and relying on spiritual belief and prayer to overcome addiction. Since the formation of AA, twelve-step programs have been established around the world for the treatment of drug addiction (Narcotics Anonymous, Cocaine Anonymous, Crystal Meth Anonymous, etc.) and have also been adapted for the treatment of compulsive behaviors (Gamblers Anonymous, Overeaters Anonymous, Sex Addicts Anonymous, etc.). Auxiliary groups have also been formed to help family members of addicts, including Al-Anon, Alateen, and Adult Children of Alcoholics. Alcoholics Anonymous remains the largest of the twelve-step programs followed by Narcotics Anonymous and Al-Anon.

Wernicke-Korsakoff syndrome: Often seen in chronic alcoholics who, due to poor health habits and alcohol use, develop a severe deficiency of vitamin B1 in their diet. In the acute stage, lack of vitamin B1 can lead to a condition known as Wernicke's encephalopathy, in which bleeding in the brain's limbic system leads to mental confusion, unsteady gait, and visual problems. Emergency treatment, including vitamin supplements, can help with the Wernicke symptoms, but the brain damage resulting from the vitamin loss typically leads to more long-term problems. The chronic stage, Korsakoff syndrome, often develops as Wernicke symptoms subside. Symptoms include severe memory problems, that is, the inability to form new memories as well as loss of many of their previous memories. They can also experience hallucinations, language and other cognitive problems. People developing this form of dementia often require long-term care since there is no known treatment.

Withdrawal symptoms: Physiological and psychological symptoms stemming from the abrupt cessation of any psychoactive substance to which someone has become addicted. Symptoms can include nausea, vomiting, rapid heart rate, diarrhea, hypertension, sweating, and tremors. While most of these symptoms are relatively mild, more severe withdrawal symptoms can also occur. Anyone experiencing auditory or visual hallucinations, seizures, mental confusion, or convulsions should seek emergency medical treatment immediately since these symptoms are often life threatening.

Zero tolerance policy: A policy implemented in many school and work settings which imposes strict punishments for the purpose of eliminating undesirable behavior. These policies prevent people in positions of authority from any kind of discretion or taking circumstances into account and can often mean a far more negative outcome as a result. Zero tolerance can apply to drug use or possession, bullying, harassment, or violence. Critics of the use of these policies in schools suggest that they lead to a "school to prison pipeline" for many students who might be treated more leniently otherwise.

Directory of Resources

WEBSITES

While most cities have local resources that can be found through your family doctor or mental health organizations, here is a list of online resources that can be accessed for more information.

Addiction Center
www.addictioncenter.com
Owned and funded by Recovery Worldwide LLC, Addiction Center operates a network of substance abuse treatment centers across the United States where people in need can get help for drug or alcohol abuse. Their website offers a round-the-clock helpline providing free help in finding substance abuse treatment programs as well as provides information on a wide range of psychoactive substances. Their online community also provides firsthand accounts of people successfully overcoming addiction and learning to move on afterward.

Medical News Today
http://www.medicalnewstoday.com/info/addiction/treatment-for-addiction.php

One of the world's best sources of information on medical issues and available treatments, Medical News Today also has a comprehensive website on addiction and treatment with information sheets on withdrawal, medical complications of addiction, and different forms that addiction can take. The site also includes a Knowledge Center outlining the latest research into addiction.

National Institute on Drug Abuse (NIDA)
https://www.drugabuse.gov/
A federal scientific research institute funded by the National Institutes of Health and the U.S. Department of Health and Human Services, NIDA is the world's largest supporter of research into drug abuse and addiction. Along with summaries of the latest research studies, NIDA's website also provides basic information on drug abuse, numerous recent publications on addiction and treatment, and links to many other organizations providing services worldwide.

Substance Abuse and Mental Health Services Administration (SAMHSA)
www.samhsa.gov
Part of the U.S. Department of Health and Human Services, SAMHSA's mission is to reduce the impact of substance abuse on communities across the United States. The SAMHSA website provides extensive information on the medical and psychological aspects of drug and alcohol abuse as well as a Behavioral Health Treatment Services Locator allowing visitors to find alcohol and drug treatment programs across the country. SAMHSA also operates a national helpline for people dealing with substance, suicidal thoughts, and disaster recovery.

U.S. Department of Veterans Affairs (VA)
https://www.mentalhealth.va.gov/res-vatreatmentprograms.asp
The VA offers a number of different treatment options for eligible veterans seeking help for substance abuse issues. Both outpatient and residential (live-in) programs are available at VA sites across the United States, where veterans can receive medically managed detoxification, family counseling, medication for psychiatric conditions, and first-time screening. Special programs are also available for women, veterans of recent deployments, and homeless veterans.

BOOKS

These are books that might be of help in dealing with substance abuse and some of the underlying issues that can be contributing to what is happening.

Brick, John (2008). *Handbook of the Medical Consequences of Alcohol and Drug Abuse*. Binghamton, NY: Routledge.

Connors, G., Donovan, D., Diclemente, C., & McCrady, B. (2001). *Substance Abuse Treatment and the Stages of Change: Selecting and Planning Interventions*. New York: Guilford Press.

Donohue, Brad & Azrin, Nathan (2012). *Treating Adolescent Substance Abuse Using Family Behavior Therapy: A Step-by-Step Approach*. Hoboken, NJ: Wiley.

Freeman, Edith M. (2001). *Substance Abuse Intervention, Prevention, Rehabilitation, and Systems Change Strategies: Helping Individuals, Families, and Groups to Empower Themselves*. New York: Columbia University Press.

Langone, J. (1995). *Tough Choices: A Book about Substance Abuse*. Boston: Little, Brown, and Company.

Newton, David E. (2010). *Substance Abuse: A Reference Handbook*. Santa Barbara, CA: ABC-CLIO.

Pagliaro, Louis A., & Pagliaro, Ann Marie. (2012). *Handbook of Child and Adolescent Drug and Substance Abuse: Pharmacological, Developmental, and Clinical Considerations*. Hoboken, NJ: Wiley.

Rivers, P. Clayton, & Shore, Elsie M. (1997). *Substance Abuse on Campus: A Handbook for College and University Personnel*. Westport, CT: Greenwood Press.

Weinstein, Sandford. (1999). *The Educator's Guide to Substance Abuse Prevention*. Mahwah, NJ: Lawrence Erlbaum Associates.

Index

About the Author

Romeo Vitelli, PhD, C.Psych., is a clinical psychologist in private practice in Toronto and Hamilton, Ontario. Prior to going into private practice, he was a staff psychologist at Millbrook Correctional Centre, a maximum-security prison in eastern Ontario, and also ran the Sex Offender treatment program in Hamilton, Ontario, for a number of years. He received his bachelor's degree from the University of Windsor and his master's and doctoral degrees from York University in Toronto, Canada. His current practice focuses on clinical neuropsychology, forensic psychology, and pain management and has treated a wide variety of disorders, including posttraumatic stress disorder, substance abuse, depression, chronic pain, and personality disorders in inpatient and outpatient settings. His other published works include *Self-Harm: Your Questions Answered* (also part of this Q&A Health Guides series) and *The Everything Guide for Overcoming PTSD*. He is also an active blogger and regular contributor to *Psychology Today* and the *Huffington Post*.